0013641

KT-216-487

1793100

The
Countryside
Handbook

B 5407

Selection and editorial material
© 1985 The Open University

Co-published by Croom Helm Ltd, Provident House,
Burrell Row, Beckenham, Kent BR3 1AT

Croom Helm Australia Pty Ltd, First Floor, 139 King
Street, Sydney, NSW 2001, Australia

Croom Helm, 51 Washington Street, Dover, New
Hampshire 03820, USA

and The Open University, Walton Hall, Milton Keynes,
MK7 6AA

British Library Cataloguing in Publication Data

The Countryside handbook.
   1. Regional planning — Great Britain — History
   — 20th century
   I. Open University   II. Great Britain.
   Countryside Commission
   711'.3'0941   HT395.G7

   ISBN 0-7099-1948-4

All rights reserved. No part of this publication may be
reproduced, stored in a retrieval system, or transmitted
in any form or by any means, electronic, mechanical,
photocopying, recording, or otherwise, without the
written permission of the Publisher.

Typeset by Leaper & Gard Ltd, Bristol
Printed and bound in Great Britain

The Countryside Handbook

The Open University in association with the Countryside Commission

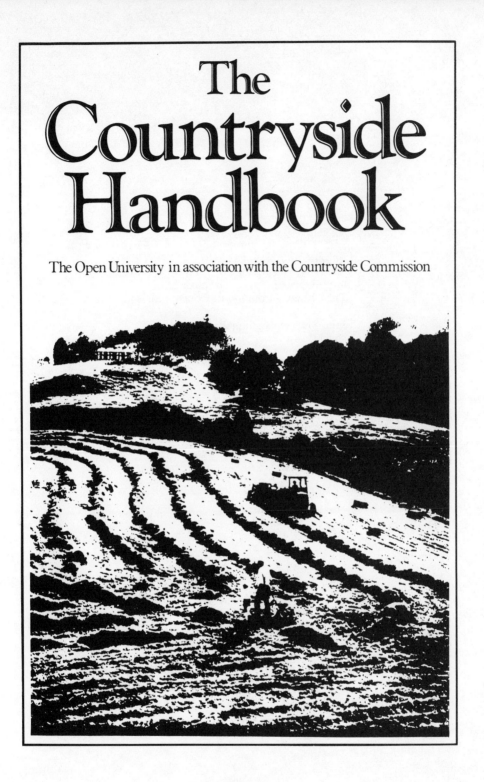

CROOM HELM
London · Sydney · Dover, New Hampshire

This book has been edited by
Alan Rogers, John Blunden and Nigel Curry
at the Open University on behalf of
The Changing Countryside Course Team:

John Blunden (Chairman)
Nigel Curry
Rees Pryce
Graham Turner (BBC)
Andrew Wood (Course Assistant)

- 34758 /5 95. 6.87

CONTENTS

Acknowledgements   viii

A Continuing Education Course from   ix
The Open University

INTRODUCTION   x

PART 1: GOVERNMENT LEGISLATION
by Louise Catchpole

SECTION 1.1: RESOURCES   3
Forestry Act 1945   3
Hill Farming Act 1946   3
Agriculture Act 1947   3
Forestry Act 1947   4
Agricultural Holdings Act 1948   4
River Boards Act 1948   5
Forestry Act 1951   5
Mineral Workings Act 1951   5
Agriculture Act 1957   5
Water Resources Act 1963   6
Commons Registration Act 1965   6
Agriculture Act 1967   6
Forestry Act 1967   7
Mineral Exploration and Investment Grant
    Act 1972   7
Water Act 1973   7
Agriculture (Miscellaneous Provisions) Act 1976   8
Forestry Act 1981   8
EEC Agricultural Directives   8

SECTION 1.2: CONSERVATION AND
RECREATION   10
Ancient Monuments Acts: Historic Buildings and
    Ancient Monuments Act 1953; Ancient
    Monuments and Archaeological Areas
    Act 1979   10
National Parks and Access to the Countryside
    Act 1949   11
Civic Amenities Act 1967   11
Countryside Act 1968   12
Nature Conservancy Council Act 1973   12
Wildlife and Countryside Act 1981   12

SECTION 1.3: PLANNING   14
Housing, Town Planning, Etc. Act 1909   14
Town and Country Planning Act 1932   14
Restriction of Ribbon Development Act 1935   14
Minister of Town and Country Planning
    Act 1943   15
Distribution of Industry Act 1945   15
New Towns Act 1946   15
Town and Country Planning Act 1947   16
Town Development Act 1952   17
Caravan Sites and Control of Development
    Act 1960   17
Town and Country Planning Act 1968   17
Town and Country Planning Act 1971   18
Local Government Act 1972   19
Community Land Act 1975   19
Local Government, Planning and Land Act 1980   20
Town and Country Planning (Minerals) Act 1981   20

SECTION 1.4: SOCIAL   21
Development and Road Improvement Funds
    Act 1909   21
Rural Water Supplies and Sewerage Act 1944   21
Mobile Homes Act 1975   21
Rent (Agriculture) Act 1976   22
Passenger Vehicles (Experimental Areas)
    Act 1977   22
Transport Act 1978   22
Housing Act 1980   23
Transport Act 1980   23
Public Passenger Vehicles Act 1981   24

PART 2: OFFICIAL BODIES
by Nigel Curry   27

SECTION 2.1: GOVERNMENTAL
AGENCIES
The European Regional and Social Funds   27

The European Commission, Directorate General for Agriculture 27

The Ministry of Agriculture, Fisheries and Food 28

The Department of the Environment 29

The Departments of Trade and Industry, Transport, Energy and The Welsh Office 30

SECTION 2.2: QUANGOS AND OTHER NATIONAL BODIES 32

The Countryside Commission for England and Wales 32

The Nature Conservancy Council 32

The Forestry Commission 33

The Development Commission 34

The English and Welsh Tourist Boards 35

The Sports Council 36

The Development Board for Rural Wales and The Welsh Development Agency 37

The Historic Buildings Councils for England and Wales 37

Significant Landowning Interests: The Royal Family, The Duchy of Cornwall, The Crown Estate Commissioners, The Church Commissioners, Oxford and Cambridge Colleges, The Aristocracy, Financial Institutions 38

The Water Sector: Water Authorities Association, Regional Water Authorities 39

The Energy Sector: The National Coal Board, The Central Electricity Generating Board, The Gas Council, The United Kingdom Atomic Energy Authority 39

SECTION 2.3: THE LOCAL AUTHORITY SECTOR 41

County Councils 41

District Councils 42

Parish and Town Councils 42

National Park Authorities 43

PART 3: PRIVATE GROUPS
by Phillip Lowe and Henry Buller

SECTION 3.1: ECONOMIC 47

The Agricultural and Allied Workers' National Trade Group of the Transport and General Workers' Union 47

The Country Landowners' Association 47

Forestry Interests in the Countryside: The Economic Forestry Group PLC, The Timber Growers United Kingdom 48

The National Farmers' Union 49

The Smallfarmers' Association 49

The Farmers' Union of Wales 50

SECTION 3.2: CONSERVATION 52

The British Trust for Conservation Volunteers 52

The Civic Trust 52

The Council for National Parks 53

The Council for the Protection of Rural England 54

Farming and Wildlife Advisory Group 55

Friends of the Earth 56

The National Trust 56

The Royal Society for Nature Conservation 57

The Royal Society for the Protection of Birds 58

Wildlife Link 59

SECTION 3.3: RECREATION 60

Field Sports Organisations: The British Association for Shooting and Conservation, The British Field Sports Society, The Game Conservancy 60

The Open Spaces Society 61

The Ramblers Association 61

Recreational Organisations in the Countryside: British Mountaineering Club, Camping and Caravanning Club, Caravan Club, Cyclists' Touring Club, Youth Hostels Association 62

SECTION 3.4: SOCIAL 64

Rural Community Councils 64

Rural Voice 65

SECTION 3.5: PROFESSIONAL 66

The Landscape Institute 66

The Royal Institution of Chartered Surveyors 66

The Royal Town Planning Institute 66

PART 4: SIGNIFICANT DOCUMENTS
by Tim Shaw

SECTION 4.1: REPORTS OF OFFICIAL COMMITTEES 71

Barlow Report 1940: Royal Commission on the Distribution of the Industrial Population 71

Uthwatt Report 1942: Expert Committee on Compensation and Betterment 72

Scott Report 1942: Committee on Land Utilisation in Rural Areas 72

Dower Report 1945: National Parks in England and Wales 73

Hobhouse Report 1947: Report of the National Parks Committee (England and Wales) 74

Skeffington Report 1969: Report on Public Participation in Planning: People and Planning 75

Sandford Report 1974: Report of the National Park Policies Review Committee 75

Dobry Report 1975: Review of the
  Development Control System   76

Stevens Report 1976: Planning Control over
  Mineral Workings   76

Verney Report 1976: Report of the Advisory
  Committee on Aggregates: The Way Ahead   77

Porchester Report 1977: A Study of Exmoor   78

Strutt Report 1978: Report of the Advisory
  Council for Agriculture and Horticulture:
  Agriculture and the Countryside   79

Northfield Report 1979: Report of the
  Committee of Inquiry into the Acquisition
  and Occupancy of Agricultural Land   80

SECTION 4.2: OTHER OFFICIAL STUDIES   81

Report of the Planning Advisory Group 1965:
  The Future of Development Plans   81

Ministry of Agriculture, Fisheries and Food 1966:
  Technical Report No. 11, Agricultural Land
  Classification   81

Forestry White Paper 1972: Forestry Policy   82

First and Second Reports of the Select
  Committee of the House of Lords on Sport
  and Leisure 1973: Sport and Leisure   83

Countryside Commission 1974: New Agricultural
  Landscapes   84

Agricultural White Papers 1975 and 1979: Food
  from Our Own Resources, Farming and the
  Nation   85

Countryside Review Committee 1976–79:
  The Countryside — Problems and Policies,
  Topic Papers 1-4   85

Countryside Commission 1976: Lake District
  Upland Management Experiment   86

Nature Conservancy Council 1977: Nature
  Conservation and Agriculture   87

Countryside Commission 1980: Areas of
  Outstanding Natural Beauty: a Policy
  Statement   88

Countryside Commission et al. 1981: Urban
  Fringe Experiment, Countryside
  Management in the Urban Fringe   89

SECTION 4.3: INDEPENDENT REPORTS
AND STUDIES   90

First and Second Land Use Surveys, 1930-49
  and 1961 onwards   90

The Countryside in 1970: Proceedings of the
  Third Conference, 1970   91

Zuckerman Report 1972: Report of the
  Commission on Mining and the Environment   91

Essex County Council 1973: A Design Guide
  for Residential Areas   92

Tourism and Recreation Research Unit 1981:
  The Economy of Rural Communities in the
  National Parks of England and Wales   93

Council for National Parks 1983: New Life for
  the Hills   93

SECTION 4.4: POLICY INSTRUMENTS   95

Ministry of Housing and Local Government
  Circular 42/55, 1955: Green Belts   95

Town and Country Planning General
  Development Order 1977, 1981,
  Statutory Instrument No. 289
  (and No. 245)   95

Town and Country Planning General
  Development Order 1977 — Article 4,
  Statutory Instrument No. 289   96

Department of the Environment Circular 22/80,
  1980: Development Control — Policy and
  Practice   97

Notes on Contributors   98

Acknowledgements

The inspiration for this book, its companion volume and the Open University course of which they are part, goes back to a series of discussions held in the late 1970s with the Countryside Commission, and it is with that organisation that we gladly begin our list of acknowledgements. We are grateful not only for the sustained and amiable dialogue that has been continued over a period of some five years with that body, but also its invaluable contribution to the financing of the overall project and upon which its ultimate fruition has so largely depended.

Whilst we were initially trying out ideas and attempting to give the subject matter an appropriate shape, we were considerably assisted in our efforts by the advice of a wide range of organisations and groups in England and Wales with an interest in rural affairs. Though most were ultimately consulted, we remain especially grateful to those who so kindly attended our consultative conference held at Walton Hall to initiate the project back in November 1981. Although the list of organisations who commented on our proposals is too long to mention in full here, it ranged from those representing important groups of users of the countryside, such as the NFU, the CLA and the Ramblers Association and ran right through to conservation groups such as the CPRE and state agencies such as the Nature Conservancy Council. The Council for Environmental Education, however, remains one group that deserves particular mention for its subsequent assistance with material prepared for registered students of 'The Changing Countryside' course.

In terms of individuals, we must single out first of all the contribution of Mary Powell who, as a former member of the Course Team, helped in the early days to grapple with the difficulties of handling the complex of interactive factors that make the countryside what it is. Hers was to be an invaluable contribution to the structure of both books and the course as a whole. Later, as the texts in question came to be written, our external assessor, Emeritus Professor Gerald Wibberley, formerly holder of the Ernest Cook chair in countryside planning held jointly at Wye College and University College in the University of London, proved a resourceful, scrupulous and tireless commentator on all that we did and has finally given his approval to *The Changing Countryside* in its book form and as an Open University course. We are also grateful to our other assessor Professor Colin Spedding of the Centre for Agricultural Strategy at the University of Reading for his comments on our efforts.

We express our thanks for the secretarial assistance given to us by Linda Charnley at the Open University and the cheerful way in which she 'word processed' our not insubstantial manuscript in a very short space of time. Our thanks also go to the thirteen people representing a variety of rural interest groups and organisations for test reading early drafts of the course materials and to Mary Geffen of the Institute of Educational Technology at the Open University. She helped us not only organise the testing programme but was instrumental in ensuring that our texts were ultimately tailored to the needs of our readers. Nevertheless, deeply as we appreciate all the efforts made on our behalf by others, we must end by fully acknowledging the fact that it is the Open University Course Team that alone bears the responsibility for all that follows.

A Continuing Education Course from The Open University

Components of the Course

This book, *The Countryside Handbook* has been published for the Open University as one element of a short course being offered under the auspices of its Continuing Education division and as part of its Personal and Cultural Education Programme. Its purpose is to act in support of the main text entitled *The Changing Countryside* which sets out to provide an account of change in the countryside, the reasons for change and the ultimate directions in which this may lead. Although *The Changing Countryside* offers an informative and stimulating experience in its own right, *The Countryside Handbook* is a useful addition for those who want to know more about the background legislation pertaining to rural areas as well as something of the organisations and other bodies that have an interest in it.

As an accompaniment to these books, BBC2 is showing a series of nine television programmes with the same title as the main text. The first programme will be shown in March 1985, the rest following in subsequent weeks. The series will be repeated in the autumn, then twice a year for the next two years with one presentation in spring 1988. Viewers will find the series offers an extremely stimulating additional dimension to the textual experience for it emphasises the visual impact on the specific rural areas of the many social and economic forces both past and present that are examined in the main text.

For those who would like, for professional or indeed personal reasons, an 'in depth' treatment of the subject matter contained in the books and the television programmes the Open University offers enrolment on 'The Changing Countryside' course itself (PD 770). This will provide opportunities for students to discuss issues raised in the main text at a day school and with their own individual tutor and undertake an assessed project in the form of a short dissertation under his or her guidance.

What Registration for the Course Offers

In addition to the two texts and the television programmes the course includes:

— a Study Guide to explain how all the parts of the course are related, including a study period timetable to help you work through the various elements
— allocation to a personal tutor who will give you detailed guidance and help in the preparation of a short project
— the opportunity to discuss issues raised in the main text at a whole-day seminar
— suggestions on how to use the course material to prepare and carry out the project work
— assessment and grading of the completed dissertation.

To enrol for it you will be required only to pay a registration fee covering tuition and course materials which are additional to the main text and companion volume which you may have already purchased. However, if you are reading this from a book you have borrowed or only have one of the two texts either can be obtained from the Open University.

How to Apply

For further information concerning the course, and television broadcasts together with an application form write to:

Associate Student Central Office
The Open University
PO Box 76
MILTON KEYNES MK7 6AA

For copies of the main text and for its companion volume, write to:

Learning Materials Services Office
Centre for Continuing Education
The Open University
PO Box 188
Walton Hall
MILTON KEYNES MK7 6DH

INTRODUCTION

The book *The Changing Countryside*, the volume associated with this Handbook, has at its heart the four themes of expanding agriculture, containing settlements, conserving nature and sustaining rural communities. In tracing out the development of these issues reference is necessarily made to the framework of legislation, the organisations both official and unofficial, and the critical documents which naturally act as the vehicles of change in the countryside. The function of this Handbook is to fill out the detail which must inevitably be omitted in the narrative of that main course text. As such it is inevitably seen too as an essential companion to the course book but it is also hoped that it will stand by itself as a valuable reference text for the growing area of countryside planning and conservation.

The four sections — Government Legislation, Official Bodies, Private Groups and Significant Documents — are broadly organised along the same lines. The objective is to give for each entry, whether law, organisation or document, a crisp pen-portrait of its background and origins, its main characteristics, a critical assessment of its significance and, in most cases, a short guide to further reading.

The choice of items for inclusion is necessarily a subjective matter though the eventual list is one compiled after discussion with many people. To some people it may at first glance seem a somewhat eclectic and even protracted list and one which pushes the theme of the changing countryside to its very limits. While it is certainly the intention to provide a comprehensive guide which will invariably give an answer to a query, this comprehensiveness is attempted for a more fundamental reason. The legal and organisational framework on which the countryside of England and Wales has developed is naturally a very broadly-based one. A proper understanding of countryside issues demands much more than knowledge of the major planning acts or the organisations involved with conservation and recreation. Most importantly, perhaps, it requires full consideration of the structures, both legal and organisational, which have created our modern agricultural industry. This point holds good for the other major resource users in the countryside too, such as forestry or the water industry. Moreover it also applies with regard to the political and administrative context within which countryside issues are framed and for the mass of often urban-based groups which increasingly regard the countryside as as much their concern as the preserve of the farmer and landowner.

A further point on this context should perhaps be made. Whereas it is certainly clear just how significant the period since the Second World War has been (Gilg's 'first three decades, 1945-76' (Gilg, 1978)) in the development of modern countryside planning, the point is also made that the antecedents of this post-war movement are much older and date back to the first decade of this century. A number of attempts have been made in recent years to structure the development of countryside issues in historical terms. Martin Shaw has shown in his introduction to the book *Rural Deprivation and Planning* (1979) how land-use problems dominated the scene until the mid-1970s when social and economic issues came to the fore. Gerald Wibberley, in his very personal view of rural planning (1983), recognised six periods, from before the Great War, through the 1920s and 1930s, the bevy of crucial reports produced in the Second World War, the reconstruction of agriculture and growth of planning in the 1940s, the boom in recreation and conservation in the 1960s to the reduced optimism and concern with conflict in the 1970s.

But overlying these quite detailed scenarios there is a more basic structure. The passing of legislation, the development of organisations and the publication of key documents while in part a gradual process, can also be seen as the product of three great radical periods in twentieth-century political life as it has affected the countryside. Interestingly each radical period has come from a different part of the political spectrum. The first, towards the end of the first decade, came from Lloyd George's reforming Liberal administration, epitomised here by the passing of the Development and Road Improvement Funds Act of 1909 (which created the Development Commission) and the Housing, Town Planning Act of the same year. The second was the fruit of the radical Labour administration of the immediate post-war years, characterised by the Town and Country Planning Act and the Agriculture Act, both of 1947. The third (though it remains to be seen whether it will be on the same scale as the others) is the retrenchment from corporatism and the influence of the state seen in the Conservative administration from 1979, here illustrated perhaps by trends towards privatisation in, for example, forestry, transport and housing.

While these periods are most obviously reflected in legislation it will also be realised that the passing of law is often only the end product of a period of developing attitudes· in society and government which are clearly illustrated by the appearance of significant documents and often also by the foundation of and then the pressure provided by an interest group. Moreover, such changes also have their implications for the structure of government and official organisations. A very clear illustration of this process, centring on the period of change immediately after the Second World War, can be seen in the case of National Parks. The build up of opinion and pressure during the 1930s, seen in the creation of the Council for Preservation of Rural England and its own creation of the Standing Committee on National Parks, was followed by the appearance of the important official reports from Dower and Hobhouse. The culmination was the passing of the National Parks and Access to the Countryside Act, 1949 and the creation of the National Parks Commission.

Just as the choice of items contained in the Handbook is inevitably a subjective one, so are the chosen items themselves the product of individual authors. While each contribution has a prime objective of providing a clear factual account, the authors have not shrunk from expressing their own critical views. Indeed the mere creation of a short pen-portrait involves an economy of style which some may think verges on the caricature and which involves the critical and selective use of material. But beyond this, the intention has been to give authors who are experienced in their respective fields the opportunity to comment frankly and dispassionately on their subject.

References

Gilg, A.W. (1978) *Countryside Planning: the First Three Decades 1945-76*, David and Charles, Newton Abbot.

Shaw, J.M. (ed.) (1979) *Rural Deprivation and Planning*, Geo Books, Norwich.

Wibberley, G.P. (1982) *Countryside Planning: a Personal Evaluation*, Occasional Paper no. 7, Department of Environmental Studies and Countryside Planning, Wye College, Ashford.

PART 1
Government Legislation

Forestry Act 1945

Background During the First World War over 400,000 acres of woodland were felled as a result of the German blockade of Britain. The Forestry Commission had been set up in 1919 to establish a strategic reserve of timber. After the Second World War a considerable acreage had again been felled or destroyed. Government policy, in a White Paper of 1943, was to increase forestry acreage, both by replanting in existing woodland areas and by planting on land which had not previously been used for forestry.

Provisions The Forestry Commission was reconstituted. The Commissioners' earlier power to acquire land compulsorily was transferred to the Minister of Agriculture. He could acquire land suited to afforestation and could also manage it himself or delegate its management to the Commission, which drew up management plans.

Comment Compulsory purchase powers have been very rarely used as there has generally been enough land available on the open market. Moreover, policy is now to relinquish publicly-held forest land.

Management plans for Forestry Commission land now cover conservation and recreation as well as forestry management.

References
HM Government (1943) *Post-war Forestry Policy*, Cmd 6447, HMSO, London

Hill Farming Act 1946

Background It was designed to increase the amount of land available for agriculture, and particularly livestock production, by assisting the rehabilitation of hill land. Special subsidies had been introduced in wartime and these were formalised in the 1946 Act.

Provisions Grants were made available for approved schemes to improve hill farming land (for example, by the erection or alteration of buildings, provision of electricity or drainage, making or improving roads or bridges, reclamation of waste land). The land had to be suitable

and the cost not unreasonably high in relation to the benefit. The original definition of 'hill farming land' was given as 'mountain, hill or heathland suitable for hardy sheep'.

Headage payments on hill sheep and cattle which had been introduced in the war were continued.

Comment Farming, though traditional, would be uneconomic in many upland areas without government subsidies and land might otherwise deteriorate to rough scrub.

The concern in this Act was entirely with issues of farm improvement and increased food supplies. Ideas on income support for farmers to keep viable populations in hill areas came later.

The Livestock Rearing Act, 1951 extended provisions to other, less disadvantaged areas.

References
Hill, B.E. and Ingersent, K.A. (1982), *An Economic Analysis of Agriculture*, 2nd edn, Ch. 9, Heinemann, London

Agriculture Act 1947

Background The Second World War and earlier trade depression suggested to many people the need for increased production of home-grown foodstuffs. Since the middle of the nineteenth century much imported food had competed on equal terms with British produce. During the Second World War food had been in short supply and had been severely rationed. The Scott Report in 1942 had advocated long-term agricultural planning to ensure stability and proper standards in the industry. The objective of the policy introduced by the 1947 Act was that of:

promoting and maintaining, by the provision of guaranteed markets and assured prices ... a stable and efficient industry capable of producing such part of the nation's food and other agricultural produce as in the national interest it is desirable to produce in the United Kingdom, and of producing it at minimum prices consistent with proper remuneration and living conditions for farmers and workers in agriculture and an adequate return on capital invested in the industry.

Provisions The Act set guaranteed minimum prices and assured markets for certain produce (for example, fat sheep and cattle, milk, eggs, wheat, barley). Prices were to be fixed after regular, annual reviews of the economic conditions and prospects of the industry. This enshrined in the Act the right of farmers to be consulted directly in the annual review and price-fixing by the Ministry of Agriculture and gave the basis of substantial power to the National Farmers' Union.

Owners and occupiers of land were required to achieve 'good husbandry' (that is, efficiency as regards kind, quantity and quality of produce). The Minister could supervise and direct farming (and, in the last resort, acquire the land) if 'good husbandry' was not achieved.

Agricultural tenants were to be compensated at the end of the tenancy by the landlord for any improvements made to the holding.

County Councils were given a duty to provide and rent out smallholdings, where a demand existed, with the intention of providing 'persons with agricultural experience an opportunity of becoming farmers on their own account'.

An Agricultural Land Commission was set up to manage Ministry-owned farmland and to advise and assist in the formulation of land management policy. County Agricultural Executive Committees were established to promote agricultural development and efficiency.

Comment The 1947 Act, though substantially modified, still sets out the basic philosophy towards agriculture which has been adopted by successive governments. Most significantly it formally committed government to intervene in agriculture in order to protect farmers from market forces.

From 1973, the substance of British agricultural policy has been based on agreed policies within Europe, notably the Common Agricultural Policy.

References
Hill, B.E. and Ingersent, K.A. (1982), *An Economic Analysis of Agriculture*, 2nd edn, Heinemann, London
Tracy, M. (1982) *Agriculture in Western Europe: Challenge and Response 1880–1980*, Granada, London

Forestry Act 1947

Background The 1945 Act had dealt with forestry on publicly-owned land. It was now intended to increase forestry projects on private land.

Provisions Landowners could enter into Forestry Dedication Covenants. These agreements meant that without the Forestry Commission's prior consent, the land could not be used other than for forestry. Financial aid was made available for the management of dedicated land (see further 1967 Act).

Comment The 'carrot' of tax concessions and grant-aid for dedicated land combined with the 'stick' of the need for felling licences in the 1951 Act. Both provisions were aimed at the encouragement of private forestry.

References
Centre for Agricultural Strategy (1980) *Strategy for the UK Forest Industry*, Report no. 6, University of Reading

Agricultural Holdings Act 1948

Background Many rules regulating the relationship of landlord and tenant of agricultural land were unwritten and long-standing customs. The custom, especially regarding tenants' rights on quitting, varied from county to county. Statutes concerning agricultural holdings had been enacted from 1875 onwards but customary rights still remained paramount.

The provisions of this Act were originally enacted as part of the Agriculture Act 1947 but became a separate statute a year later.

Provisions The Act applied to the letting of agricultural land used for the purposes of a trade or business and effectively gave a tenant life-long security provided he remained solvent and paid his rent.

The tenant could refer the terms of the tenancy to an arbitrator if he had no agreement in writing with the landlord. The arbitrator then fixed an agreement on terms reached by landlord and tenant.

Tenancies of two years and more could only be terminated by between one and two years notice by either party.

Rent variations made at the time the tenancy was renewed could be referred to arbitration.

The tenant was bound to manage and use the farm in a 'husbandlike manner' in accordance with the custom of the county where it was situated. (So local customs as to a particular system of farming were to be followed unless the landlord gave other more precise instructions as to cultivation.)

At least twelve months' notice to quit was to be given. The tenant could then appeal to the Agricultural Land Tribunal unless, for example, he had broken an obligation under the tenancy regarding cultivation or payment of rent. Compensation was payable to the tenant at the end of the tenancy for improvements he had made to the holding. Cases of dispute could be referred to the Agricultural Land Tribunal.

Where a tenancy was ended by notice to quit the tenant was entitled to compensation for disturbance of one year's rent (or more if more actual loss could be proved).

Comment The Act contained important provisions which remained virtually unaltered for many years, although changes have recently been effected.

One significant alteration in 1976 gave a close relative of a deceased tenant the right to apply to the Agricultural Land Tribunal to take over the holding on the same terms. (See Agriculture (Miscellaneous Provisions) Act, 1976.)

References
Gregory, M. and Parrish, M. (1980), *Essential Law for Landowners and Farmers*, Granada, London

River Boards Act 1948

Background Local authorities had been given powers to control river pollution in the nineteenth century, though these powers were little used and authorities themselves were often the main pollution offenders.

Provisions A system of 32 river boards was created, based on drainage basin boundaries.

Powers over water abstraction, land drainage, fisheries and river pollution were given to river boards.

Comment Powers over pollution were further strengthened by the Rivers (Prevention of Pollution) Act, 1951.

The River Boards used most of their resources on pollution prevention; they had no power to carry out construction works.

Public water supply remained independent of the Boards and in the hands of water companies.

References
Parker, D.J. and Penning-Rowsell, E.C. (1981), *Water Planning in Britain*, Allen and Unwin, London

Forestry Act 1951

Background As with previous legislation this Act had the prime aim of ensuring the establishment and maintenance of adequate reserves of growing trees.

Provisions Felling of trees, except under licence, was prohibited.

Licences, obtainable from the Forestry Commissioners, could be subject to conditions that the land was restocked or other land was planted instead.

No licence was needed for 'lopping' or 'topping', or for certain types of trees; for example, fruit trees and trees less than a certain diameter.

Compensation was available if refusal of a licence caused deterioration.

Commissioners could undertake direct felling where necessary. If felling would cause the owner a net loss he could require the Commissioners to buy the trees or the Minister to buy the land where they were growing.

Comment Some overlap is evident between felling controls and Tree Preservation Orders. Felling controls were originally designed to maintain adequate reserves of growing timber, but both came to be exercised in the interests of amenity.

A Tree Preservation Order under the Town and Country Planning legislation is overridden by a felling licence.

The power to undertake direct felling was re-enacted in the 1967 Forestry Act but has not been used.

References
Centre for Agricultural Strategy (1980), *Strategy for the UK Forest Industry*, Report no. 6, University of Reading

Mineral Workings Act 1951

Background The working of minerals constitutes 'development' in planning terms and, therefore, requires planning permission. This Act made it possible for conditions to be put in planning permissions for rehabilitation of worked-out land.

Provisions A fund was set up to finance the restoration of worked-out ironstone land with both operators and central government making contributions to the fund.

Payments were made to operators for levelling or other work to restore the fertility of worked-out land. Part of the cost of each project was to be borne by the operator himself.

Comment The Act only applied to workings started after 1951, so much land which was worked out after 1951, and where workings had begun earlier, was not covered.

References
Blunden, J. (1975), *The Mineral Resources of Britain*, Hutchinson, London

Agriculture Act 1957

Background Farmers had been pressing for a limitation on the freedom of government to reduce guaranteed prices in the annual review.

Provisions Most importantly, the Act made special provision to ensure stability of prices during each 'guarantee' period.

The government agreed not to reduce prices by more than a given percentage in each year and by not more than 9 per cent over any three-year period for livestock products (for example, milk).

Requirements could be imposed that products were distinctively marked and subjected to inspection and marketing controls.

Wool was added to the list of products in the 1947 Act with guaranteed prices and assured markets.

Government grants were made available towards the cost of long-term improvements to agricultural land, including erection and improvement of farm buildings, provision of electricity, etc. One-third of reasonable cost was to be generally payable.

Grants were also made available to facilitate the formation of economic agricultural units. Up to one-third of surveyors' fees, legal fees, etc. were payable.

Comment In practice, the Act probably did little to prevent a decline in real prices through inflation, particularly since the powers given under the 1947 Agriculture Act still allowed government to limit commodities which were eligible for guarantee.

The major significance of the Act for the countryside probably lies in the support which it gave to improvements in agricultural land and buildings.

References

Hill, B.E. and Ingersent, K.A. (1982), *An Economic Analysis of Agriculture*, 2nd edn, Heinemann, London

Water Resources Act 1963

Background The Proudfoot Committee had been set up to investigate the growing demand for water and had reported in 1962. It concluded that a body was needed to co-ordinate national water supply and pollution control and to provide guidance to reorganised water authorities.

Provisions River Authorities were set up in England and Wales, to deal with groups of river basins rather than individual rivers.

The Authorities were to take over the pollution control functions of the old River Boards and also to be responsible for control and planning of water resources in their areas. Powers were given to carry out engineering works to remedy predicted supply deficiencies.

The Water Resources Board was set up as a central co-ordinating body to manage national resources.

Comment The measures were found not to be sufficiently comprehensive. Pressure on resources became such that small area authorities could no longer cope and the need for multi-purpose regional authorities became clear during the 1960s.

References

Parker, D.J. and Penning-Rowsell, E.C. (1981), *Water Planning in Britain*, Allen and Unwin, London

Proudfoot, J. (1962) *Final Report: Central Advisory Water Committee, Sub-Committee on the growing demand for water*, HMSO, London

Commons Registration Act 1965

Background Common land totalling over 600,000 hectares is a major land resource in Britain. Its location, extent and the rights claimed over it needed to be accurately recorded, yet these factors were often imperfectly known.

Provisions Registers were to be made by local authorities of all common land and town and village greens and all rights of common claimed by 1970.

The completed register was to be conclusive evidence of all the matters in it. Where ownership of the land was not claimed, ownership of a town or village green would be vested in the local authority, but unclaimed common land would just be placed under the protection of the local authority.

Procedures for disputing registration were created.

The New Forest, Epping Forest and the Forest of Dean were exempted from the Act.

Comment Registration was to be completed by 1970, but in fact the process and disputes over land ownership and rights of grazing continued for many years afterwards.

References

Denman, D.R., Roberts, R.A. and Smith, H.J.F. (1967) *Commons and Village Greens*, Leonard Hill, London

Stamp, L.D. and Hoskins, W.G. (1963) *The Common Lands of England and Wales*, Collins, London

Agriculture Act 1967

Background A growing concern in agriculture had been the plight of the small farmer. A Government White Paper in 1965 proposed assistance by encouraging the enlargement and amalgamation of farm holdings and co-operation in farming and marketing. This Act was seen as a means of legislating to support the small farmer.

Provisions Grants were made available for farm amalgamations and boundary adjustments designed to create commercial agricultural units; one-half of expenditure could be claimed. Additional loans were available to cover costs and the purchase price of any land acquired.

Lump sum or annuity grants were payable to individuals relinquishing the occupation of uncommercial agricultural units in the Payment to Outgoers Scheme.

A new grants system (replacing that in the 1957 Act) for long-term improvements to agricultural land was introduced. Costs had to be reasonable in relation to the benefit in farming achieved and one-quarter of costs could be met.

Additional grants were made available for improvements to hill land designed to increase productivity.

Provision was made for an entirely new regional agency, the Rural Development Board, to balance agricultural against other needs. Rural Development Boards were to deal with the Act's provisions relating to hill land in areas where special problems of balance between agricultural and other needs existed. Boards were to draw up programmes for their area and to implement them by grant and loan assistance and to promote farm amalgamations and boundary adjustments.

Comment The major innovation was the provision for Rural Development Boards. In fact only one was set up (North Pennines Rural Development Board) and this lasted less than two years, though a second Rural Development Board had been planned for Wales. Policy changes following the Conservative electoral victory in 1969 brought an end to the experiment.

The structural components of the Act in many ways provided the blueprint for the Common Market directive of 1972 on structural policy in agriculture.

The Farm Amalgamations and Boundary Adjustments Scheme and the Payments to Outgoers Scheme which were part of this Act proved less popular than was expected. Restrictions for 40 years on the sale of parts of a farm which had been enlarged under the schemes were subsequently reduced to 15 years by the Agriculture Act 1970 and then to five years in the Agriculture (Miscellaneous Provisions) Act 1972.

References

Childs, G. and Minay, C.L. (1977) *The Northern Pennines Rural Development Board*, Oxford Polytechnic, Department of Town Planning

Hill, B.E. and Ingersent, K.A. (1982) *An Economic Analysis of Agriculture*, 2nd edn, Heinemann, London

House, J.W. (1976) *The Geographer and Policy Making in Marginal Rural Areas: the Northern Pennines Rural Development Board* in Coppock, J.T. and Sewell, W.R.D. (eds), *Spatial Dimensions of Public Policy*, Pergamon Press, Oxford

Forestry Act 1967

Background This consolidated and re-enacted earlier legislation.

Provisions Various schemes to assist private landowners with forestry projects were introduced as follows.

Dedication Agreements — giving comprehensive control and restricting land use to the growing of timber in accordance with an agreed long-term plan of operations. Grant aid was made available for planting and for management. Felling licences were not needed and Tree Preservation Orders could not apply.

Approved Woodland Schemes — for landowners not wishing to part with rights of management in the long term. Planting grants were made available for planting in accordance with an agreed scheme but no financial help with later management.

Small Woods Planting Grants — similar to the Approved Woodland Scheme, grants were made available for small areas of land suitable for tree planting.

The provisions regarding felling licences were re-enacted. Conditional licences were introduced, requiring replanting only where necessary for forestry, agriculture or the amenities of the district.

Where there was failure to comply with a conditional licence, specified steps to remedy the default could be required.

The Act set up the Home Grown Timber Advisory Committee to advise the Commission, promote forestry interests and link the Commission with private interests.

Comment Conditional licences requiring replanting were used only where grant aid would be available. The procedures for enforcing conditions are similar to the enforcement notice procedure in the Town and Country Planning Act 1971. It has proved difficult to apply in this context;

a simple monetary penalty might possibly be more appropriate.

The 1972 White Paper on forestry considered that forestry dedication schemes with their complex administrative arrangements, were impractical and should fall into disuse, but new schemes have since been announced.

References

Centre for Agricultural Strategy (1980) *Strategy for the UK Forest Industry*, Report no. 6, University of Reading

Mineral Exploration and Investment Grant Act 1972

Background Investment grants to encourage mineral exploration had been withdrawn in 1970. This Act was designed to provide financial assistance for the early stages of exploration when financial risk was greatest.

Provisions The Act authorised financial assistance towards the costs of searching for, or (on discovery), validating mineral deposits.

Exploration had to be carried out with planning permission, where it was needed.

A sum of £50 million was set aside. Not more than 35 per cent of costs were to be paid.

Comment Pre-1970 conditions were not really restored. Other factors, the state of international markets and regional investment grants, had more effect on the impetus to explore for minerals.

References

Blunden, J. (1975) *The Mineral Resources of Britain*, Hutchinson, London

Water Act 1973

Background The Act stemmed from recommendations made by the Central Advisory Water Committee. There had been a number of different water authorities, with differing responsibilities — river authorities, water undertakings and sewerage and sewage disposal authorities. The all-purpose authorities set up under the Act were intended to increase efficiency and reduce duplication of effort.

Provisions Nine regional water authorities in England together with the Welsh National Water Development Authority were created having a duty to supply water within their areas.

The National Water Council was formed to assist discussion between regional water authorities and the formulation of a common view.

Water authorities were to be responsible not only for water supply, sewerage and sewage disposal but also for land drainage, control of river pollution and recreational use of inland waterways (excluding canals). These aspects are often dealt with by other bodies under licence.

A duty was given to water authorities to have regard to the desirability of conservation and of preserving natural beauty in their areas and to the need to preserve public access to places of natural beauty.

The Water Space Amenity Commission was created to review progress in development of water space for amenity and recreation.

Comment The Act came into force, along with local government reform, on 1 April 1974.

Water authorities are still primarily concerned with water supply and environmental issues tend to take second place.

Water authority areas do not necessarily coincide with local authority areas, a factor which can lead to conflicts in development policy.

Twenty per cent of water supply is still provided by private companies.

The National Water Council and the Water Space Amenity Commission were subsequently disbanded.

References
Parker, D.J. and Penning-Rowsell, E.C. (1981) *Water Planning in Britain*, Allen and Unwin, London

Agriculture (Miscellaneous Provisions) Act 1976

Background Tenant farmers, particularly through the National Farmers' Union, had for long argued for amendments to the Agricultural Holdings Act 1948 to give greater security of tenure for the families of tenants.

A scheme allowing family succession was included in a miscellaneous statute in 1976. Its hasty inclusion (believed by some to have been conceded in exchange for legislation on tied cottages in the same year) and consequent poor drafting, has caused many problems since enactment.

Provisions Relevant provisions are to be found in Part II of the Act.

On the death of a sole (or sole-surviving) tenant, relatives may apply within three months to the Agricultural Land Tribunal for permission to succeed to the tenancy. The Tribunal must be satisfied of the eligibility of the applicant and that any claim by the landlord for repossession of the holding is not stronger than the claim for tenancy succession.

The applicant, to be eligible, must be a close relative (wife, husband, brother, sister or child), have received, for at least five of the previous seven years, his principal source of livelihood from the holding and must not be the occupier of another commercial unit.

Only two successions to the tenancy are allowed under the Act.

Comment Despite the obvious benefit of this legislation to existing tenants and their families, there has been growing concern about this Act since it was passed. The trend nationally towards owner occupation has reduced the number of available tenancies and this Act has served to reduce the flow even more.

Consequent upon growing pressure for reform, a bill is presently (March 1984) passing through Parliament which if enacted would remove the automatic right of succession for family members.

References
Gregory, M. and Parrish, M. (1980) *Essential Law for Landowners and Farmers*, Granada, London

Forestry Act 1981

Background Policy changes consequent upon a change of government in 1979 favoured increasing privatisation of forestry. Financial pressures also encouraged the sale of publicly-owned forest land.

Provisions Powers were given to Ministers to sell forestry land (except in the Forest of Dean).

In exercising the powers, regard had to be given to the national interest in maintaining and expanding national forestry resources.

Comment The Act facilitated Government policy to encourage private participation in forestry.

It was intended to raise some £40 million between 1981 and 1984 by sales. Social, economic and conservation matters had to be taken into account in determining areas for sale, though this has not prevented significant concern by some conservation interests and rural lobbyists. In practice the level of sales has been below that expected.

References
Centre for Agricultural Strategy (1980) *Strategy for the UK Forest Industry*, University of Reading
Montgomery, D. (1981) 'Forestry and the Environment', *Countryside Planning Yearbook*, Geo Books, Norwich

EEC Agricultural Directives

Background Article 39 of the Treaty of Rome (1957) states:

(1) The objectives of the Common Agricultural Policy shall be:

(a) to increase agricultural productivity by promoting technical progress and by ensuring the rational development of agricultural production and the optimum utilisation of the factors of production, in particular labour;

(b) thus to ensure a fair standard of living for the agricultural community, in particular by increasing the individual earnings of persons engaged in agriculture;

(c) to stabilise markets;

(d) to assure the availability of supplies;

(e) to ensure that supplies reach consumers at reasonable prices.

(2) In working out the Common Agricultural Policy and the special methods for its application, account shall be taken of:

(a) the particular nature of agricultural activity, which results from the social structure of agriculture and from structural and natural disparities between the various agricultural regions;

(b) the need to effect the appropriate adjustments by degrees;

(c) the fact that in the Member States agriculture constitutes a sector closely linked with the economy as a whole.

The three principles of the Common Agricultural Policy may be considered as: common prices, Community preference and financial solidarity. The major element in the Policy concerns the Markets policy. This takes over 90 per cent of total CAP spending and is generally enforced through the medium of binding Community regulations.

The Structural policy of the CAP, while only involving a relatively small amount of expenditure, is of particular concern for broad countryside, as opposed to strictly agricultural, purposes. It is generally enforced by directives which are far less binding and precise than regulations. In particular, it should be noted that directives may be 'interpreted' by national governments and, in this regard, it is noticeable that while the Less-Favoured Areas Directive has been enthusiastically adopted by the British government, that on socio-economic advice has received relatively little attention.

Provisions *Directive 71/159* — a subsidy given to farmers to carry out a development plan. Aid was selective and applicants needed to show they could achieve incomes comparable with other occupations.

Directive 72/160 — a complementary scheme to give financial incentives to elderly farmers to retire and release their land, generally to 'development plan' farmers.

Directive 72/161 — to provide farm families with socio-economic information, including advice on non-farming opportunities and to set up training courses to enable agricultural workers to learn new skills and improve existing ones.

Directive 72/268 — concerned less-favoured areas (affected by climate and/or terrain and thus liable to depopulation and decline in agricultural activity). It introduced an allowance for farmers in such areas and offered preferential terms for investment.

Comment Development plan and retirement schemes have generally been little used, largely because of the comparable income requirement.

The impact of socio-economic advice and training schemes has again been small in England and Wales. Most training courses are for fairly basic skills. A new provision was made later for training managers of agricultural co-operatives.

Grants to less-favoured areas have extended existing UK hill farming grant schemes, though there is evidence that this has mainly been to the benefit of larger farmers.

Directives have a limited life and are due to be changed.

References

Harris, S., Swinbank, A. and Wilkinson, G. (1983) *The Food and Farm Policy of the European Community*, Wiley, Chichester

Lasok, D. (1980) *The Law of the Economy in the European Communities*, Ch. 12, Butterworth, London

Marsh, J.S. and Swanney, P.J. (1980) *Agriculture and The European Community*, Allen and Unwin, London

Tracy, M. (1983) *People and Politics in Rural Development*, Arkleton Trust

Tracy, M. (1982) *Agriculture in Western Europe: Challenge and Response, 1880--1980*, Granada, London

Section 1.2
CONSERVATION AND RECREATION

Ancient Monuments Acts

Background Protection was first given to ancient monuments in 1882. Then 50 monuments were specifically protected. Now more than 12,000 monuments are protected.

The Secretary of State for Environment has the duty to schedule as ancient monuments buildings or structures above or below ground whose preservation is of national importance because of their historic, architectural, traditional, artistic or archaeological interest.

Occupied houses and buildings in ecclesiastical use could not be scheduled. Protection of buildings in regular use is much more recent, with protection first given in 1932. A building can be both a scheduled monument and a listed building. Generally a monument is a site not in current use whilst a listed building is occupied. Listing is a relatively quick process; scheduling taking longer. A building may thus be first listed and later scheduled.

Historic Buildings and Ancient Monuments Act 1953

Provisions The Historic Building Councils for England, Wales and Scotland were established.

Power was given to the Secretary of State to make grants for the repair of buildings of outstanding historical or architectural interest. Grants could be subject to conditions. (Since 1967 it has been possible to make loans for these purposes.)

Power was given to the Secretary of State to make grants to local authorities and the National Trust for the acquisition of properties of historic or architectural interest.

Provisions in relation to ancient monuments were superseded by the 1979 Act.

Comment Other sources of grant-aid for the upkeep of historic buildings are the National Heritage Fund (whose trustees can make grants or loans for the acquisition, maintenance or preservation of buildings, etc.) and grants and loans from local authorities (available since 1962).

Ancient Monuments and Archaeological Areas Act 1979

Provisions The Act requires the Secretary of State to compile and maintain a schedule of monuments (including all monuments scheduled under earlier legislation).

New controls were introduced over carrying out works to a scheduled monument. Consent of the Secretary of State is needed for any works but there are certain excepted categories (for example, agricultural and horticultural works previously carried out on the same site). If consent is refused, compensation is payable only if the works did not amount to 'development' (under the Town and Country Planning Act 1971) or were in accordance with a planning permission granted before the monument was scheduled or were reasonably necessary for the continued use of the monument.

Power was given to the Secretary of State to have the guardianship of a scheduled monument with the owner's consent and to take over responsibility for maintenance and management.

Compulsory purchase is possible, where the owner of a scheduled monument is not fulfilling his responsibility to maintain it.

Power was given to the Secretary of State and local authorities to designate areas as being of archaeological importance. In a designated area anyone planning to carry out operations disturbing the ground is required to give six weeks' notice to the local authoritiy. After inspection of the site it could be required that the site should be excavated before the operations are carried out. A period of up to four months excavation is permitted.

Comment These provisions are designed to operate quickly and wherever possible, to foster goodwill with owners and occupiers of scheduled monuments.

References
Haynes, J.S. (1983) *Historic Landscape Conservation*, Gloucestershire Papers in Local and Rural Planning, no. 20, Gloucestershire College of Arts and Technology, July

National Parks and Access to the Countryside Act 1949

Background Setting up National Parks had first been recommended in 1931 and the Scott Report (1942) regarded their establishment as overdue. In 1945 the Dower Report defined National Parks as extensive areas of beautiful and relatively wild countryside. Priorities were to be conservation and public access yet maintaining established farm use. The Hobhouse Report (1947) followed these recommendations and suggested twelve sites, all but two of which (the Norfolk Broads and the South Downs) were later approved.

The Act gave no order of precedence to conservation, recreation and local economic enterprises.

Provisions A National Parks Commission (later to become the Countryside Commission) was created. Its functions were:

(1) to have an overall duty for preservation and enhancement of natural beauty throughout the country, although especially in relation to National Parks and Areas of Outstanding Natural Beauty;
(2) to encourage the provision of facilities for the enjoyment of National Parks;
(3) to designate National Parks;
(4) to designate Areas of Outstanding Natural Beauty;
(5) to give advice and assistance to local authorities.

Any land in a National Park could be acquired by agreement or compulsory purchase order to give the public access to it for outdoor recreation.

Nature reserves could be established by local authorities or by the Nature Conservancy (now the Nature Conservancy Council). Reserves would be established by agreement with the landowner (who received compensation for the restrictions imposed) or, if necessary, compulsorily.

County councils had a duty to survey their areas to discover what public rights of way existed and to incorporate them in a map to be reviewed every five years. Provision for the establishment of special long-distance routes to be used by walkers, horse riders and cyclists. Routes could be over existing or new rights of way and land could be acquired compulsorily where necessary.

County councils were also required to survey their areas to discover the extent of 'open country' (areas 'wholly or predominantly of mountain, moor, heath, down, cliff or foreshore') and to decide whether it was necessary to secure public access to it. A map of 'open country' in each area was to be published with steps to secure access described. Access agreements were to be reached with a landowner, or if necessary access orders were to be made with compensation payable to the landowner. Local authorities were given power to acquire open country in their area by compulsory purchase to secure public access to it.

Certain 'exempted land' could be covered by an access agreement but not an access order. This included, for example, agricultural land other than rough grazing, land covered by buildings and land declared as nature reserve, park or garden land, golf courses.

Comment The Act attempted to cover too many diverse matters and was less successful than it should have been as a result. The organisations set up by the Act were left short of manpower and resources to do their work. Various subsequent statutes (for example, the Countryside Act 1968, the Nature Conservancy Council Act 1973, the Wildlife and Countryside Act 1981) have altered arrangements commenced by the 1949 Act. Most importantly conflicts between conservation, public access and agriculture were created and have not been resolved.

The Act remains, however, the essential starting point of post-war conservation/designation attempts.

References
Cherry, G.E. (1975) *National Parks and Recreation in the Countryside. Environmental Planning 1939–1969* Vol. II, HMSO, London
Dower, J. (1945) *National Parks in England and Wales,* Cmnd 6628, HMSO, London
Garner, J.F. (1974) *Rights of Way and Access to the Countryside,* Oyez Practice Notes no. 55, Oyez Publishing, London
HMSO (1947) *National Parks (England and Wales): Report of the Committee* (Hobhouse Report), Cmnd 7121
McEwen, A. and McEwen, M. (1982) *National Parks: Conservation or Cosmetics?,* Allen and Unwin, London

Civic Amenities Act 1967

Background Previously individual monuments or buildings only could be listed or scheduled, not whole groups of buildings and their surroundings. The Civic Amenities Act was designed to remedy this deficiency.

Provisions A local authority could designate as a conservation area any area of architectural or historic interest which should be preserved or enhanced in character or appearance.

If the area contained listed buildings or scheduled monuments, those protections would continue to operate in relation to those buildings.

Willful damage to a listed building was made an offence.

The local authority was empowered to carry out urgent works to preserve an unoccupied listed building.

Conditions requiring tree planting and tree preservation orders were to be made, where necessary, on granting applications for planning permission.

Comment All these provisions were subsequently re-enacted in the Town and Country Planning Act, 1971 which made further provision for conservation areas.

References
Bingham, D.A. (1973) *The Law and Administration Relating to Protection of the Environment,* Oyez Publishing, London

Countryside Act 1968

Background Recreational pressure on the countryside increased vastly after the passage of the 1949 Act. A 1966 Government White Paper proposed changes to cope with the expected growth in pressure to use the countryside in future. It was felt that the functions of the National Parks Commission needed to be broadened so that the whole countryside would be covered.

A parallel statute in Scotland (the Countryside Commission (Scotland) Act 1967) set up the Scottish Countryside Commission. Pressure on wild areas there had been much less severe.

Provisions The Countryside Commission was constituted (in place of the National Parks Commission) with a broader role to be concerned with the conservation and enhancement of the countryside and the encouragement of provision of facilities for people going to the countryside for recreation.

Local authorities and private individuals were given powers to provide Country Parks and picnic sites — places in country surroundings, not necessarily beauty spots, for the enjoyment of the countryside by the public.

Authorities were given a duty, in exercising functions in relation to land, to have regard to the desirability of conserving the natural beauty and amenity of the countryside.

Powers were conferred on highway authorities to signpost any public footpath or bridleway and required them to signpost where the path leaves a metalled road and wherever necessary to assist those wishing to follow it.

Comment This Act effectively updated both the ideas behind the 1949 Act and the administrative structures set up to implement them. It reflected in part ideas current in the 1960s on the likely future growth of recreation which had been highlighted in Michael Dower's *Fourth Wave*.

The possible conflicts between the Commission's duties in respect of recreation and conservation were in general not foreseen. Equally unrecognised at the time was the question of the social and economic interests of inhabitants within National Parks.

Local authorities had also a duty to have regard to the needs of agriculture and forestry and the economic and social interests of rural areas. This was likely to counterbalance the general duty under this Act.

References
Cherry, G.E. (1975) *National Parks and Recreation in the Countryside. Environmental Planning 1939–1969*, Vol. II, HMSO, London
Dower, M. (1965) *Fourth Wave: the Challenge of Leisure*, Civic Trust, London
HMSO (1966) *Leisure in the Countryside*, Cmnd 2928
Patmore, J.A. (1983) *Recreation and Resources: Leisure Patterns and Leisure Places*, Blackwell, Oxford

Nature Conservancy Council Act 1973

Background In 1965 the Nature Conservancy (set up in 1949) had become part of the Natural Environment Research Council. It had been short of funds as a result, and was felt by many to be less effective.

Provisions The Nature Conservancy Council was established as an independent body, funded by the Department of the Environment, and given three main functions:

— to advise Ministers on nature conservation policy and to provide advice and information generally on nature conservation;
— to establish and manage nature reserves;
— to encourage research into conservation.

The Nature Conservancy Council was given various functions in relation to Sites of Special Scientific Interest (see Wildlife and Countryside Act, 1981).

Comment In practice the research function was given over to the newly created Institute of Terrestrial Ecology leaving the Nature Conservancy Council with the major roles of giving advice and managing resources.

Funding for the activities of the Nature Conservancy Council is still felt by many to be too low, particularly since the increased pressures consequent upon the Wildlife and Countryside Act, 1981.

The Council still lacks an overall land use policy and has, therefore, tended to work through isolated conservation projects and *ad hoc* responses to issues as they arise.

References
Department of the Environment (1974) *Nature Conservation*, Circular 161/74, HMSO, London
Green, B.H. (1981) *Countryside Conservation*, Allen and Unwin, London

Wildlife and Countryside Act 1981

Background A Countryside Bill promoted by the Labour administration fell when the Conservative government came to power in 1979. When the Wildlife and Countryside Bill was introduced into the House of Lords it was described as a compromise between the competing interests of agriculture and conservation; subsequently it was regarded by many conservationists as a victory for the agricultural lobby.

Provisions The Nature Conservancy Council was required to notify local planning authorities, owners and occupiers of any land of special scientific interest within their area. Notification entailed describing the operations which would be likely to damage those special features.

Owners or occupiers of such land seeking to carry out damaging operations had to apply to the Nature Conservancy Council to obtain permission. A wait of three months after notification was then necessary (that is, the NCC was not able to *prevent* damaging operations).

Special protection was given for certain 'super-SSSIs'. Where damaging operations were proposed, the NCC could instead offer to buy the land or make payments to the owner to preserve it. Such an offer prevented the owner carrying out the operations for twelve months. During that period the land could be acquired compulsorily if no agreement with the owner had been reached.

Compensation was payable to the landowner where the creation of a super-SSSI had reduced the value of an interest in agricultural land.

Where an application for a farm capital grant (under the Agriculture Act, 1970) concerned land which was an SSSI any objections by the NCC have to be taken into account. If, as a result, the application is refused, the NCC has to offer to enter into a management agreement with payments to the landowner.

Powers were given to the Secretary of State or local authorities to make a 'limestone pavement order' prohibiting disturbance or removal of limestone in any area of special interest.

Powers were given to NCC to declare land of national importance as a National Nature Reserve.

Powers were given to NCC to make grants for expenditure on anything conducive to nature conservation.

Powers were given to planning authorities to enter into management agreements with landowners for the purpose of conserving or enhancing the land's natural beauty or amenity. Such management agreements could limit the use to which the land was put and compensation payments where land use was restricted must be paid by the authority to the landowner.

Powers were introduced to restrict ploughing and other operations on moor and heath land in National Parks. Notice of such operations has to be given to the county planning authority whose consent is needed. Alternatively operations may go ahead after three months without a decision or twelve months after a refusal of permission. Management agreements are likely to be made where permission is refused.

Comment The provision concerning refusal of farm capital grants and the entitlement to compensation forced the NCC to enter into management agreements in such cases. Conservation measures were thus weakened and no extra finance provided to cover this expenditure. There is a distinct danger that objections will not be made to farm grant applications because no funds are available to pay the resulting compensation.

In a similar vein super-SSSIs are also likely to cause compensation payments to be made in many cases. Funds are short for this and even shorter for the alternative of compulsory purchase.

Many provisions depend on voluntary agreements and co-operation by the landowner. The extent of real co-operation remains to be seen and in many ways the onus to prove the success of voluntary agreements through the Act now lies with farmers and landowners.

Parliamentary debates on the Act had stretched over eleven months. There had been considerable lobbying beforehand when various consultation papers were issued but environmental groups had not always been well-prepared with their arguments.

References

Cox, G. and Lowe, P. (1983) 'A Battle Not the War: the Politics of the Wildlife and Countryside Act', *Countryside Planning Yearbook*, Geo Books, Norwich

Denyer Green, B. (1983) *The Wildlife and Countryside Act 1981: the Practitioner's Companion*, Surveyors Publications, London

HAROLD BRIDGES LIBRARY
S. MARTIN'S COLLEGE
LANCASTER

PLANNING

Housing, Town Planning, Etc. Act 1909

Background Nineteenth century statutes had set standards for public health and housing. These had been concerned with individual buildings rather than the relationship of buildings to each other. This was the first Act to legislate in a comprehensive way which would today be regarded as planning. In the words of John Burns, President of the Local Government Board, when he introduced the Bill, it was intended to secure 'the home healthy, the house beautiful, the town pleasant, the city dignified and the suburb salubrious'.

Provisions Local authorities were given powers to make town planning schemes for land being used or likely to be used for building.

Schemes were intended to secure 'proper sanitary conditions, amenity and convenience in connection with the laying out and use of the land, and of any neighbouring lands'.

Schemes needed approval from the Local Government Board. They could be enforced by the removal or alteration of any building or work in contravention.

Comment The machinery for the making and approval of schemes proved too complicated and later legislation simplified the procedure.

In 1919 under the provisions of the Housing and Town Planning Act a duty was imposed on local authorities with a population over 20,000 to prepare schemes.

References
Cherry, G.E. (1974) *The Evolution of British Town Planning*, Leonard Hill, London
Heap, D. (1982) *An Outline of Planning Law*, Sweet and Maxwell, London

Town and Country Planning Act 1932

Background This repealed all the earlier statutes dealing with town planning and re-enacted the law in consolidated form and with various significant changes.

Provisions Authorities could for the first time draw up schemes covering land which was likely to be developed.

Planning schemes confirmed by the Minister of Health were binding both on local authorities and on developers.

Before a scheme, development could take place under an Interim Development Order. If that development later contravened the scheme, the developer would receive compensation.

Comments There was no duty to draw up schemes and so many authorities did not do so.

The process for drawing up or changing a scheme was very lengthy and complicated involving years of preparation and parliamentary approval for schemes. The system was, therefore, unpopular.

References
Cherry, G.E. (1974) *The Evolution of British Town Planning*, Leonard Hill, London
Cullingworth, J.B. (1982) *Town and Country Planning in Britain*, Allen and Unwin, London
Heap, D. (1982) *An Outline of Planning Law*, Sweet and Maxwell, London

Restriction of Ribbon Development Act 1935

Background The Town and Country Planning Act 1932 had enabled local authorities to prepare planning schemes but was not mandatory. Unsightly and uncontrolled development along new or improved roads had proved a particular problem and this Act sought to tackle the problem of ribbon development.

Provisions New building within 220 feet of classified roads was made subject to planning control.

Other roads could be covered by the same control if made the subject of a resolution under the Act.

Comment Piecemeal control proved unsatisfactory and, therefore, by 1943, all land was made subject to planning control.

References
Heap, D. (1982) *An Outline of Planning Law*, Sweet and Maxwell, London

Cherry, G.E. (1974) *The Evolution of British Town Planning*, Leonard Hill, London

Cullingworth, J.B. (1982) *Town and Country Planning in Britain*, Allen and Unwin, London

Minister of Town and Country Planning Act 1943

Background The central authority in planning matters had previously been the Ministry of Health. In 1942 most responsibilities were transferred to the Minister of Works and Planning and a year later another change was made.

Provisions The post of Minister of Town and Country Planning was created.

The Minister was charged with the duty to secure consistency and continuity in the framing and execution of a national policy for land use and development.

Planning responsibilities under all earlier legislation were transferred to the new Minister.

Comment The new Ministry, to concentrate solely on planning matters, was short-lived. In 1951 the title changed again first to the Ministry of Local Government and Planning and then to Ministry of Housing and Local Government.

The Secretary of State for the Environment (currently the Minister responsible) has acquired wide statutory powers to control land use in pursuance of the policy first set out in the 1943 Act.

References

Cherry, G.E. (1974) *The Evolution of British Town Planning*, Leonard Hill, London

Cullingworth, J.B. (1982) *Town and Country Planning in Britain*, Allen and Unwin, London

Cullingworth, J.B. (1975) *Reconstruction and Land Use Planning 1939–47, Environmental Planning 1939–1969*, Vol. I, HMSO, London

Heap, D. (1982) *An Outline of Planning Law*, Sweet and Maxwell, London

Distribution of Industry Act 1945

Background The concern for the declining economies of the old industrial areas and for the adverse effects of the distribution of manufacturing industry had led to the publication of the Barlow Report in 1943. This Act was designed to provide comprehensive controls over the distribution of industry.

The Act was the first major piece of post-war legislation in the area of environmental and economic planning. The controls necessarily applied during wartime and the boost to manufacturing industry provided by the war acted as an impetus to the introduction of post-war direction.

Provisions The Act created Development Areas in which the Board of Trade could acquire land and construct buildings for industrial purposes. The creation of the new Development Areas meant that the Special Areas (designated under Acts of 1934 and 1937) were repealed.

The Act allowed the Board of Trade to make loans to companies in Development Areas to provide premises and to improve basic services.

All new industrial construction had to be notified to the Board of Trade under the terms of the building licence system, unless the floor area was less than 10,000 sq feet (these limits were subsequently modified).

New industrial premises, irrespective of the requirement to have Board of Trade permission, had to comply with planning legislation.

Comments The Development Areas recognised in the Act were North East England, West Cumberland, South Wales and Monmouthshire and Central Scotland. Other areas (for example, North East Lancashire, Merseyside) were subsequently added.

The control of industrial construction under the building licence system which had been introduced during the war was replaced in 1948 (under the provision of the Town and Country Planning Act 1947) by the requirement to obtain an Industrial Development Certificate for buildings in excess of 5,000 sq. feet.

While the Act appeared a concerted attempt to tackle problems of industrial growth and distribution, it had several failings. The controls applied to manufacturing industries only. The Barlow Commission had underestimated the likely growth of the service industries and it was these which were subsequently shown to grow while manufacturing declined.

Incentives for industrial investment in the Development Areas were mainly in the form of financial aid for capital. This did not tackle the problems of employment and may even have exacerbated them as manufacturers were encouraged to replace men with machines.

While the Act probably did help industrial investment in the Development Areas, it did nothing to deflect employment growth from the more prosperous areas of the South East and the Midlands.

References

Keeble, D. (1976) *Industrial Location and Planning in the United Kingdom*, Methuen, London

New Towns Act 1946

Background The new towns movement began in 1897 when Ebenezer Howard published his book *Tomorrow: a Peaceful Path to Real Reform*, later republished as *Garden Cities of Tomorrow*. A Garden Cities Association was formed and two voluntary building experiments were carried out at Letchworth and Welwyn.

The importance of garden cities was recognised in various pre-war planning statutes which gave power to the Minister to acquire land for a garden city development by compulsory purchase.

The Barlow Committee regarded urban decentralisation as a priority. Rebuilding older, war-damaged towns was seen as likely to cause overspill problems which should be planned for. A New Towns Committee under the chairmanship of Lord Reith was appointed to report on the organisation and planning principles involved with implementing a new towns programme.

Provisions Sites were to be designated as 'new towns' where the Minister deemed it 'expedient in the national interest'.

Each designated site had to have a development corporation with powers to manage and build on land or to dispose of it for others to develop.

The Corporations' activities were to be financed by central government and their proposals for development were to be subject to ministerial approval.

Ministerial direction could be given, where necessary, to ensure the preservation of any features of special architectural or historic interest, and, in particular, of listed buildings.

Comment This Act provided the basis for the eventual designation of 30 new towns in Britain. Subsequent legislation in 1965 brought together the 1946 Act with some later amendments.

When the development of particular new towns was completed, the assets administered by the new town corporation were transferred to the Commission for New Towns.

The wide powers available to the Secretary of State to direct both the Commission for New Towns and individual development corporations have been used since 1980 to require them to sell new town assets and effectively to privatise the new towns.

References

Barlow, M. (1940) *Report of the Royal Commission on the Distribution of the Industrial Population*, Cmd 6153, HMSO, London

Cherry, G.E. (1974) *The Evolution of British Town Planning*, Leonard Hill, London

Cullingworth, J.B. (1979) *New Towns Policy, Environmental Planning 1939–1969*, Vol. I, HMSO, London

Reith, J. (1946) *Report of the New Towns Committee*, Cmd 6876, HMSO, London

Town and Country Planning Act 1947

Background Haphazard development, particularly between the wars, and a rapidly increasing population had led to a serious loss of agricultural land, as well as of areas of natural beauty.

It was felt that town planning schemes did not relate to each other and so the general question of population grouping throughout the country had not been considered.

Three government committees had examined the problems:

— the *Barlow Committee* noted the dangers of swollen and unplanned towns and the loss of agricultural land.

Effective regional planning and the development of garden cities and similar projects had been recommended;

— the *Scott Report* considered land use in rural areas and suggested a presumption of agricultural use for agricultural land and more effective control over development;

— the *Uthwatt Committee* examined the problem of betterment and compensation resulting from control of land use and recommended the taxation of development gains made from planning consents.

Provisions County councils and county borough councils were made local planning authorities with a duty to survey their area and examine social and economic, as well as physical, factors.

Planning authorities were required to produce a development plan to be based on the results of the survey. The plan was to show proposals for land use in the area and the stages by which it was proposed that development would be carried out.

A new survey and review of the plan was required every five years.

No development could take place without planning permission. In deciding whether to grant planning permission for development the local planning authority would take into account the development plan and any other material considerations. The development plan itself did not give any rights to develop.

Where planning permission was refused or granted subject to conditions, no compensation was generally payable. However, if land became incapable of any reasonable beneficial use, the owner could serve a purchase notice requiring the authority to buy it.

Comment The 1947 Act remains the prime piece of legislation which sets out the British system of planning. Subsequent amendments and re-enactments have not materially affected the philosophy contained with the Act.

Ownership of land no longer carried an automatic right to develop. A £300 million fund was set up to compensate landowners for the loss of development value expropriated by the state. This scheme was later greatly altered as a result of change of government.

The development plan system was intended to be very flexible but in practice became very rigid. Plans took too long to revise, and so many five year reviews did not take place.

In retrospect, it has been argued that the system tended to overemphasise physical land use patterns at the expense of social objectives.

References

Cherry, G.E. (1974) *The Evolution of British Town Planning*, Leonard Hill, London

Cullingworth, J.B. (1975) *Reconstruction and Land Use Planning 1939–47, Environmental Planning 1939–1969*, Vol. I, HMSO, London

Heap, D. (1982) *Outline of Planning Law*, Sweet and Maxwell, London

McAuslan, P. (1975) *Land Law and Planning*, Weiden-feld and Nicolson, London

Telling, A.E. (1982) *Planning Law and Procedure*, Butterworth, London

Town Development Act 1952

Background Problems of urban overspill which had been recognised by the Barlow Commission resulted in pressure to formalise population dispersal. The resulting scheme was viewed as complementary to the new towns scheme. The Act was designed, by increasing the size of existing towns, to relieve overpopulation elsewhere, particularly in the larger cities.

Provisions Local authorities were authorised to enter into agreements for town development schemes between an 'exporting' and 'receiving' authority.

The scheme had to be a substantial one, providing for the relief of congestion or overpopulation in an area outside the county in which the development was to be carried out.

The 'receiving' authority carrying out the development could gain substantial grants from central funds and approval might also be given by the government for the making of grants by the 'exporting' authority.

A special housing subsidy, payable for ten years, was also available. The amount of the subsidy and any conditions were entirely matters for ministerial descretion.

Comment About 60 agreements were made under the Act, at least half of which were completed.

A review of dispersal policy in the mid-1970s resulted in a reduction in scale of remaining schemes. By 1978 most remaining schemes involved the Greater London Council. However, the importance of revitalising the London docklands and other inner city areas was increasingly recognised and it was decided that the remaining GLC schemes should be terminated as quickly as possible. In 1981 a five-year period was announced to end the 16 final GLC schemes. The powers of county councils to enter into further agreements had been taken away by Local Government, Planning and Land Act, 1980.

References

Cherry, G.E. (1974) *The Evolution of British Town Planning*, Leonard Hill, London

Cullingworth, J.B. (1982) *Town and Country Planning in Britain*, Allen and Unwin, London

Heap, D. (1982) *An Outline of Planning Law*, Sweet and Maxwell, London

Caravan Sites and Control of Development Act 1960

Background The Town and Country Planning Act, 1947 had been relatively ineffective in dealing with caravans and many caravan sites were operating without planning permission.

Demands for statutory control involved a licensing system which was intended to supplement planning controls. The planning issues concerned the effect of use as a caravan site on the land itself and on the surrounding area, while the licensing provisions were concerned with the internal arrangements of the site and its facilities.

Provisions A site licence was required wherever caravans were being used for human habitation, though there were various exceptions (for example, a caravan in the garden of a house or the temporary stationing of a caravan).

The site licence could be granted only where planning permission had already been obtained for the use of the site for caravans. If the planning permission was of temporary duration then the site licence would be also.

Wide discretion was given to the local authority to attach conditions to a site licence, concerning, for example, the restriction of numbers or sizes of caravans, direction as to positioning, enhancement or preservation of the amenity of the site by tree planting, fire prevention measures, etc.

Any conditions had to relate to the physical use of the land and could not, for example, set the rents of occupiers.

Model standards set by the Secretary of State were to be taken into account by local authorities in determining licence conditions.

It was possible to introduce a condition requiring a reduction in the number of caravans on an existing site, but the number could not be required to fall below that in the Secretary of State's model standards. The local authority had to be satisfied that suitable alternative accommodation was available for any displaced residents.

Any development required to be carried out by conditions in a site licence did not need planning permission.

Comment Although licensing was concerned with the internal arrangements of a site, it still related only to the physical use and appearance of the land.

Very real problems remained in the relationship between the site owner and the caravan occupier and attempts were subsequently made to solve these in the Mobile Homes Acts, 1975 and 1983.

References

Cullingworth, J.B. (1982) *Town and Country Planning in Britain*, Allen and Unwin, London

Heap, D. (1982) *An Outline of Planning Law*, Sweet and Maxwell, London

Telling, A.E. (1982) *Planning Law and Procedure*, Butterworth, London

Town and Country Planning Act 1968

Background After 20 years of operation the 1947 scheme was seen to have various defects. Procedures were slow and cumbersome; there was too little opportunity for individual participation in the planning process and the system was one of negative control on undesirable development rather than positive encouragement to good planning.

A Planning Advisory Group report argued for a radical change in the form and content of development plans, with less central government control of plans.

Provisions An overall structure plan, and consequential local plans, would together constitute the development plan.

A survey should be conducted by the local planning authority prior to drawing up the structure plan. The survey was to cover physical and economic factors, the distribution of population, transportation and traffic.

Structure plans were written statements of policy and proposals for the area. Structure plans were required to contain broad general policies and proposals relating to planning but not, for instance, statements of social policy.

Structure plans should be drawn up by individual counties or neighbouring counties working together.

There should be considerable public consultation and discussion during the drawing up of a plan.

Comment The structure plan/local plan system was subsequently re-enacted in the 1971 Act and is thus still the operative system.

References

Alder, J. (1979) *Development Control*, Sweet and Maxwell, London

Cullingworth, J.B. (1982) *Town and Country Planning in Britain*, Allen and Unwin, London

Elson, M. (1981) 'Structure Plan Policies for Pressured Rural Areas', *Countryside Planning Yearbook*, Geo Books, Norwich

Heap, D. (1982) *An Outline of Planning Law*, Sweet and Maxwell, London

Jowell, J. and Noble, D. (1981) 'Structure Plans as Instruments of Social and Economic Policy', *Journal of Planning and Environment Law, 466*, 466–80

Planning Advisory Group (1965) *The Future of Development Plans*, HMSO, London

Telling, A.E. (1982) *Planning Law and Procedure*, Butterworth, London

Town and Country Planning Act 1971

Background This Act amended the 1968 Act and brought together much of the earlier legislation.

Although much of the basic system had remained unaltered since 1947, the 1971 Act became the main statute and provided the framework for all town and country planning regulation.

Provisions *Development Plans.* The structure plan, a written statement of policy, proposals for improvements of the area and indications of any action areas for comprehensive improvement, together with any local plans, form the development plan. Structure plans were subject to the approval of the Secretary of State. Opportunities had to be given to interested bodies to make representations before the plan was drawn up and the plan had to be advertised and opportunities provided for objections. Local plans had to be produced to supplement the structure plan. These local plans could be: district plans (comprehensive proposals for a particular area); action area plans (where, within ten years, a programme of development, redevelopment or improvement was planned); or subject plans (a detailed treatment of, for example, transport in the area). Local plans had to be accompanied by scale maps and contain specific proposals. They were to be drawn up after local consultation, allowing opportunities for objection, but the final approval of a plan was by the local planning authority itself (unless 'called in' by the Secretary of State).

'Development' requiring planning permission was defined as 'the carrying out of building, engineering, mining or other operations in, on, over or under land, or the making of any material change in the use of any buildings or other land'. Two main categories of development were recognised — 'operations' and 'changes of use'. An operation involved changing the physical characteristics of the land, while a change of use required planning permission only where it was material (i.e. substantial) in altering the character of the land.

Enforcement notices were to be issued where development occurred without planning permission. These specified the development, the steps required to put matters right and the period for compliance. No enforcement notice was needed where planning permission would have been given if it had been sought. Fines would be levied for failure to comply with an enforcement notice, and the planning authority could enter the land, carry out the work and charge the owner.

Tree preservation orders could be made for a single tree or a group, prohibiting felling or other damaging operations without the consent of the local planning authority.

Section 52 agreements. Section 52 of the Act gave powers to local planning authorities to enter into agreements with landowners restricting or regulating their development or use of land. Such agreements would be enforceable against subsequent owners since they would operate as restrictive covenants on the land.

Conservation areas. Special publicity was to be given to applications for planning permission in conservation areas, both on the site and in local newspapers. Demolition (not generally considered as development) needed special permission. If buildings were listed, regard had to be taken of the special character of the buildings. If buildings were not listed, then the effect on the whole conservation area had to be considered.

Listed buildings. Special consent was required for any works of alteration to listed buildings. Even where the work did not amount to development, consent was needed where it affected the building's character.

Comment This Act, while subsequently altered in some respects, remains the major and seminal statute concerning town and country planning.

References

Alder, J. (1979) *Development Control*, Sweet and Maxwell, London

Cullingworth, J.B. (1982) *Town and Country Planning in Britain*, Allen and Unwin, London

Denyer Green, B. (1982) *Development and Planning Law*, Estates Gazette, London

Heap, D. (1982) *An Outline of Planning Law*, Sweet and Maxwell, London

Telling, A.E. (1982) *Planning Law and Procedure*, Butterworth, London

Local Government Act 1972

Background Local authorities had been set up in the nineteenth century and their functions and boundaries had since become less appropriate to the needs of planning and administration.

Local authorities were split into (rural) County Councils, (urban) County Boroughs and Rural Districts, and thus disputes over land were frequently polarised on an urban-rural basis.

The Redcliffe-Maud Report on local government had recommended a system of unitary authorities but with a change of government these proposals were not implemented. Instead a new two-tier system was introduced by this Act.

Provisions New structures for local government were created in England and Wales; these came into effect on 1 April 1974.

A two-tier system of County and District councils was introduced. Districts were much larger than the County Boroughs and Rural Districts and were given direct responsibility for planning matters. Major conurbations were to be administered by Metropolitan Counties.

Counties were to act as county planning authorities and Districts as district planning authorities. Joint planning boards could be set up by the Secretary of State as County or District planning authorities.

County planning authorities were to be responsible for the structure plan and for certain 'county matters' regarding the control of development (for example, applications for mineral working and for development partly inside and partly outside a National Park).

District planning authorities were to be responsible for preparing local plans within their area and for the control of development under the Town and Country Planning Act, 1971. There were detailed provisions to ensure that district planning authorities would consult the relevant county planning authority where an application for planning permission concerned development conflicting with policies or proposals in the structure plan.

Comment Debate has continued since enactment on the advisability of a two-tier system. Subsequent legislation has resulted in district councils taking on more responsibility for planning matters.

Recent government action makes it increasingly likely that the large metropolitan county councils will be abolished.

References

Dearlove, J. (1979) *The Reorganisation of British Local Government*, Cambridge University Press, Cambridge

Heap, D. (1982) *An Outline of Planning Law*, Sweet and Maxwell, London

Redcliffe-Maud (1969) *Local Government in England 1966-9*, Report of the Royal Commission, Cmnd 4040, HMSO, London

Telling, A.E. (1982) *Planning Law and Procedure*, Butterworth, London

Community Land Act 1975

Background Over many years attempts had been made to recover betterment (the enhancing of property value as a result of some central or local government action) by direct charge on the property owner, by reducing compensation paid on compulsory acquisition of land or by purchase of the land at its previous value and resale at a price reflecting betterment.

The Uthwatt Report had recommended the nationalisation of development rights in land outside built-up areas. The Community Land Act was a more radical attempt to solve the betterment problem.

Provisions Local authorities in England and a central Land Authority for Wales had to draw up schemes of land acquisition and management, deciding which land in their area was needed for development within a ten-year period.

Local authorities first had power to acquire land for relevant development; eventually there was to be a duty to acquire land.

When the development value of land was realised a development land tax was payable. If the land was acquired compulsorily the authority would deduct the tax from the compensation paid.

At the future time when local authorities were to have a duty to acquire land, development value would be excluded altogether from compulsory purchase compensation and only current use value would be paid. Development land tax, therefore, was seen only as a temporary measure until the later stage.

When an authority acquired land it could develop it itself or sell it at a price reflecting development value. All major development land was intended eventually to be, or to have been, in local authority ownership.

Under the provisions of the Act a local authority could, if it saw fit, grant itself planning permission for land which it had acquired.

Comment Provisions of the Act were slow to take effect as the development market was stagnant at the time.

A change of Government caused the Act to be repealed by the Local Government, Planning and Land Act, 1980.

The Land Authority for Wales was subsequently retained but with limited powers. It had to dispose of land for development and could not grant itself planning permission.

References

Cullingworth, J.B. (1982) *Town and Country Planning in Britain*, Allen and Unwin, London

Heap, D. (1982) *An Outline of Planning Law*, Sweet and Maxwell, London

McAuslan, P. (1975) *Land Law and Planning*, Weidenfeld and Nicolson, London

Telling, A.E. (1982) *Planning Law and Procedure*, Butterworth, London

Local Government, Planning and Land Act 1980

Background A huge and complex statute with the avowed aim of fostering better relations between central and local government and between councillors, officials and the communities they served.

Provisions District planning authorities were given more freedom in determining what should be 'county matters' as regards planning applications and on which consultation with the County planning authority was necessary. The final decision on such applications should lie with the District planning authority but the general objectives of the structure plan should be taken into account.

An expedited procedure was introduced for local plans, so that they could, if necessary, come into force before the structure plan for the area.

Powers were given to the Secretary of State to set a scale of charges for planning applications. No extra fee was payable for planning appeals nor certain other applications (for example, listed building consent) but the fee would not be refunded if the application was unsuccessful.

The Community Land Act, 1975 was repealed, but many of its provisions were re-enacted in Wales. The Land Authority for Wales was retained with a duty to acquire land needed to be made available for development and to dispose of it to others for that development.

Powers were given to the Secretary of State to direct a local authority to make an assessment of land in its area which is available and suitable for development.

Power was given to the Secretary of State to compile a register of land, owned by various public bodies, which it considered to be unused or insufficiently used. Once registered by the Secretary of State the sale of the land could be ordered.

Comment The Act was considered by many authorities to be too wide-ranging to have any clear overall direction.

The relationship between District and County planning authorities was delineated. Neither were given increased powers but the decision and consultation system was intended to be speeded up with less duplication of work.

The Act expedited the local plan procedure with the result that plans could be made without a public inquiry.

The Community Land Act had been controversial and it was perhaps inevitable that it would be short-lived. The development land tax was retained to ensure some community share in development values.

It had been suggested that unused land in private ownership should also be registered but it was considered that such land was subject to special disciplines (for example, high interest rates and the consequent cost of keeping land unproductive) and so the proposal came to nothing.

References

Catchpole, L.D. (1982) 'The Local Government Planning and Land Act 1980', *Countryside Planning Yearbook*, Geo Books, Norwich

Cullingworth, J.B. (1982) *Town and Country Planning in Britain*, Allen and Unwin, London

Denyer Green, B. (1982) *Development and Planning Law*, Estates Gazette, London

Heap, D. (1982) *An Outline of Planning Law*, Sweet and Maxwell, London

Telling, A.E. (1982) *Planning Law and Procedure*, Butterworth, London

Town and Country Planning (Minerals) Act 1981

Background The Act implemented some recommendations of the 1976 Stevens Report on planning control over mineral working, notably those suggesting stricter planning controls.

Provisions The County planning authority was to be the 'mineral planning authority' with a duty to make regular reviews of areas which have been, are being or are to be used for mineral working. Following a review, the authority could revoke or modify a planning permission or prevent further working of the land.

Conditions in planning permissions could cover not just the restoration of the land but also 'aftercare' (making the land suitable for agriculture, forestry or amenity).

The normal duration of a mineral planning permission should be 60 years.

Comment The 'aftercare' period (normally about five years after restoration) was designed to ensure that not merely cosmetic restoration was carried out. However, 'aftercare' conditions are likely to be difficult to enforce.

References

Roberts, P.W. and Shaw, T. (1982) *Mineral Resources in Regional and Strategic Planning*, Gower, Aldershot

Stevens, R. (1976) *Planning Control and Mineral Workings*, HMSO, London

Development and Road Improvement Funds Act 1909

Background A concern for rural welfare in Lloyd George's Liberal administration resulted in the creation of a Development Fund.

Provisions A Development Commission, originally of five members, was set up to make grants or loans to non-profit making bodies on application and to frame its own schemes.

Powers were given to make advances to aid and develop agricultural and rural industries by research and experiment, to reclaim and drain land, to improve rural transport, to aid forestry and for any other purpose to advance economic development.

A Development Fund was to be created receiving £500,000 per year for five years from 1911 from central funds and to be at the disposal of the Commission.

The Development Commission was given power to acquire land compulsorily where needed for an approved scheme.

Comment An Act of same name in 1910 increased the number of Commissioners to eight.

Many of the Commission's original functions (notably agricultural development and research) are now covered by specific legislation and other organisations.

Subsequently the Development Commission developed its work in two main directions: rural industries have been encouraged through the Rural Industries Bureau (to 1968) and subsequently the Council for Small Industries in Rural Areas; rural community development has been encouraged through the work of county-based Rural Community Councils which are substantially funded by the Development Commission.

Under the provisions of the Miscellaneous Financial Provisions Act, 1983, the Development Commission became (with effect from April 1984) a grant-in-aid body. The Act effectively replaced the Acts of 1909 and 1910.

References
Clarkson, S. (1980) *Jobs in the Countryside*, Occasional Paper no. 2, Department of Environmental Studies and Countryside Planning, Wye College, Ashford

Development Commission *Annual Reports*, HMSO, London
Hodge, I. and Whitby, M. (1981) *Rural Employment. Trends, Options, Choices*, Methuen, London

Rural Water Supplies and Sewerage Act 1944

Background The extent of poor water supplies and sewerage services in rural Britain had been highlighted by the Scott Report. The capital cost of water supply had previously been met by the local community and the shortage of money had frequently resulted in poor service.

Provisions The Minister was enabled to contribute towards the expenses of the water authority in providing a supply of water or improving an existing supply in a rural locality.

Payments could also be made for the sewerage or disposal of sewage in a rural locality.

Grants could be made either by lump sum or by periodical payment over not more than 30 years.

Comment A long-lasting scheme with a real effect on water supply in rural areas.

References
Parker, D.J. and Penning-Rowsell, E.C. (1981) *Water Planning in Britain*, Allen and Unwin, London

Mobile Homes Act 1975

Background The Act was designed as a temporary measure covering occupiers of caravans on 'protected sites'; that is, sites licensed under the 1960 Caravan Sites and Control of Development Act. Previously there had been much concern that some site owners had too frequently misused their position and had overcharged tenants, and forced them to purchase their mobile homes at expensive rates of interest, etc.

Provisions The owner of a caravan site had a duty to offer to enter into an agreement with a person stationing a caravan there as his only or main residence.

Such agreements were to be for terms of five years and to contain particulars of charges payable, undertakings (for example, as to services provided and repairs) and the rights of respective parties. Such agreements were binding on successors in title of the parties.

An owner failing to offer to enter into an agreement could have a standard agreement forced upon him.

The Secretary of State was given power to prescribe minimum standards in regard to layout, facilities, services and equipment of 'protected sites'.

Comment The Act had a huge weakness in that the site-owner only had to 'offer to enter into an agreement' rather than being obliged to enter into one, a position altered by the 1983 Act.

The Secretary of State, in fact, never used his power to lay down minimum standards.

References
Department of the Environment (1977) *Mobile Homes in England and Wales, 1975*, HMSO, London

Rent (Agriculture) Act 1976

Background A farmer previously had an automatic right to a possession order in respect of a tied cottage (that is, one which went with the job), but the order could be deferred for up to six months unless farming would be seriously prejudiced.

This Act altered the tied cottage system to extend a broad equivalent to a Rent Act code to agricultural workers.

It was intended to ensure that no farmworker could be evicted until alternative accommodation was available and to detach in part farmworkers' conditions of employment from their housing.

Provisions A person occupying a house under a contract was to be termed a 'protected occupier'; after the contract ended occupation could continue as a 'statutory tenant'.

Security of tenure was to be similar to the Rent Act security (that is, no eviction without suitable alternative accommodation provided by the landlord or local authority) unless a term of the agreement (for example, regarding the condition of the property or payment of rent) had been broken.

The terms of occupation and rent payable by 'statutory tenants' were laid down.

The landlord could not get possession from an ex-employee in order to house a new one.

When accommodation was needed for a replacement worker and the farmer had no alternative accommodation but rehousing was appropriate in the interests of farming, a duty fell on the local authority to endeavour to provide suitable alternative accommodation.

Agricultural Dwelling-house Advisory Committees were set up to advise farmers and local authorities where rehousing was sought.

Comment The Act did not apply to Forestry Commission workers nor to casual workers or seasonal workers.

Generally two years' whole-time work in agriculture (less an allowance of 13 weeks for unemployment etc.) was necessary to qualify for Act protection. Workers disabled through industrial injury did not need to have completed two years.

The Act seems to have worked fairly well so far although total abolition of the tied cottage system is still sought by the farm workers' union.

References
Irving, B.L. and Hilgendorf, E.L. (1975) *Tied Cottages in British Agriculture*, Tavistock Institute for Human Relations, London
Gregory, M. and Parrish, M. (1980) *Essential Law for Landowners and Farmers*, Granada, London

Passenger Vehicles (Experimental Areas) Act 1977

Background The continued concern over rural transport problems led to an attempt to institute experiments where the normal licensing controls on public transport were removed.

Provisions A total of 16 rural transport experiments (RUTEX) were set up by the Department of Transport in Devon, North Yorkshire, Dyfed and Ayrshire to study the meeting of transport needs in various rural areas.

RUTEX schemes were to last two years (with a possible two-year extension). Within each designated area the law relating to public service vehicles could be modified by the local authority. This authorisation could permit small private or commercial vehicles to carry fare-paying passengers without complying with the normal legal requirements.

References
Planning Exchange (1979) *Rural Transport Experiments*, Planning Exchange, Glasgow
Transport and Road Research Laboratory (1980) *The Rural Transport Experiments*, Proceedings of a symposium held at the Transport and Road Research Laboratory, Report no. 584, TRRL

Transport Act 1978

Background A need was recognised to plan integrated public transport more comprehensively in rural areas. Previous legislation (notably the Local Government Act 1972) had introduced a requirement for local authorities to produce an annual Transport Policy and Programme which would form the basis for the allocation of the Transport Supplementary Grant. Metropolitan counties had particularly benefited and the 1978 Act was an attempt to shift the balance slightly towards rural areas.

Provisions Non-metropolitan County Councils were

given the duty to prepare and publish five-year Public Passenger Transport Plans and to review the plan every twelve months.

The plan was to cover the county, assessing community needs and the extent to which they had already been met, and to set out objectives and financial proposals to deal with unmet need.

Local authorities were given a duty to develop policies promoting co-ordinated and efficient public passenger transport and to promote any necessary amalgamation and reorganisation.

Government agreed to subsidise at least half the cost of all off-peak travel by the elderly, blind and disabled.

Comment Provisions appear to have had little effect. Many authorities have limited transport planning experience and are reluctant to support public transport. The element of social planning implicit in this Act was largely removed by the passing of the Transport Act 1980 and its greater concern for economic criteria.

References
Department of Transport (1978) *Innovation in Rural Bus Services*, Eighth Report from the Select Committee on Nationalised Industries, HC635, HMSO, London
Rigby, J.P. (1980) *Public Transport Planning in Shire Counties*, Department of Town Planning, Oxford Polytechnic, Oxford

Housing Act 1980

Background This was a major attempt by a Conservative Government elected in 1979 to reduce state influence within housing provision. Public sector housing tenants (especially council house tenants) were enabled by the Act to buy their houses. Councils previously had a discretion to sell, but many rural authorities had been reluctant to sell especially where council house numbers were small.

Provisions This imposed a minimum qualifying period of three years as a tenant of a local authority before the right to buy was available.

The tenant paid the market price less a discount according to the length of his residence (a basic 33 per cent discount for minimum qualifying period of three years then 1 per cent up to a maximum of 50 per cent).

If the house to be bought under the Act was in a National Park, an Area of Outstanding Natural Beauty or a designated 'rural area' (under Section 19 of the Act), conditions could be imposed restricting the rights of resale of the house. These conditions could require the resale or lease to someone who had lived or worked in the area in question for the preceding three years or sale back to the authority if the purchaser wished to move within ten years. The selling authority could choose what form of condition to impose.

Comment It is estimated that 400,000 households had taken advantage of the right to buy by 1983.

A large number of rural areas (*c.* 150) sought designation, although, only a small proportion (22) succeeded.

The operation of the special rural protection is likely to be hampered by the embarrassment to a council of buying back, at a higher price, a house sold at a discount, and the consequent reluctance of the housing authority to enter into an agreement.

References
Clark, D. (1981) *Rural Housing Initiatives*, National Council for Voluntary Organisations, London
Phillips, D. and Williams, A. (1983) 'The Social Implications of Rural Housing Policy: a Review of Developments in the Last Decade', *Countryside Planning Yearbook*, Geo Books, Norwich

Transport Act 1980

Background A major policy change in transport provision was consequent upon the election of a Conservative government determined to increase the private involvement in transport provision. As public transport diminished, so policy was switched to encouraging small-scale private transport schemes especially in rural areas.

Provisions The Act's most radical change was the deregulation of many public transport services. Smaller vehicles (less than eight seats) no longer required public passenger licences.

The Act allowed private minibus or car-sharing schemes. Journeys were not to be regarded as made in the course of a business of carrying passengers if their fares did not exceed the actual cost of the journey.

The Minister was given the power to designate 'trial areas' where no road service licence was needed for local public services.

School buses could be used as local fare-paying bus services both during and after the times of their school transportation function.

Ordinary car insurance policies were to be valid for car-sharing schemes.

Road service licences were no longer required for long distance bus services (over 48 kilometres).

Comment There has been some feeling that car-sharing schemes would draw passengers from conventional bus routes and thus undermine their stability.

The provision removing road service licences from long distance routes has led to a substantial increase in intercity bus schemes. While this has no immediate effect upon rural transport, there is concern that in the longer term the trend will remove traffic from the railways, thus reducing their overall viability, and will also 'cream off' more profitable long distance routes which might previously have helped support less profitable rural services.

References
Rigby, J.P. (1980) *Public Transport Planning in Shire Counties*, Department of Town Planning, Oxford Polytechnic, Oxford

Public Passenger Vehicles Act 1981

Background It consolidated and re-enacted much of the earlier legislation, including the 1978 Act provisions concerning fare-paying passengers on school buses.

Provisions Community bus services (provided to meet a community's social and welfare needs, without a view to profit and where the driver was paid only expenses) were exempted from various Act requirements. These included the need for the driver to have a public service vehicle licence and for the bus to have a certificate of vehicle fitness.

Comment A minor contribution to the solution of rural transport problems.

PART 2
Official Bodies

GOVERNMENTAL AGENCIES

The European Regional and Social Funds

Background Both of these EEC Funds provide a framework for Britain's existing regional and social policies. The Regional Fund comprises 4.9 per cent of the EEC budget as a whole, and the Social Fund makes up 4.1 per cent (agriculture made up 67 per cent in 1983). There is a significant allocation of both funds in the countryside.

Constitution The Social Fund was set up in 1958 under Articles 123–8 of the Treaty of Rome. It was reformed in 1971 to counter unemployment generally within the EEC, and to be more project-specific. It was reformed again in 1978 to focus more on less developed areas and to speed up the application process for grants.

The Social Fund's purpose is to assist in the training and retraining of young workers, migrant workers, textile workers, the handicapped and those leaving agriculture, particularly in regions of structural and technical change. It promotes worker mobility between jobs and regions.

The Regional Development Fund was established in 1975 to correct regional imbalances arising from industrial change, structural underdevelopment, and specifically regional imbalances arising out of agricultural policy. The focus of grant-aid has been on industrial and infrastructure projects in less developed regions. The Regional Development Fund was reformed in 1979 to introduce both quota and quota-free sections of the fund (see below).

Workings The Social Fund is applied for through the Social Fund Advisory Committee who advise the European Commission on allocations in accordance with project priorities. In 1980 Britain received £135 million, or 27 per cent, of the fund. Although a proportion of this was spent in rural areas, the majority, £48 million, was spent on the Youth Opportunities Programme.

The Regional Fund operates in two ways: quota and non-quota sections. The former is project-specific with grants of up to 50 per cent of national public contributions. Grants are applied for to the Commission within a grant allocation for each country, but projects must be given a priority by national governments and must fall within a development programme region (which includes remoter rural areas). In 1980, Britain received 23.8 per

cent of the quota fund. Over £550 million has been received in aid since 1975. Kielder Reservoir (Northumberland), the largest reservoir in Europe, attracted a grant of £65 million.

The Regional Fund non-quota section is aimed at being more comprehensive across the EEC policies. Funding is for overall development programmes rather than specific projects, but in 1980, this section was restricted to 5 per cent of the Fund as a whole. The first non-quota programme in Britain has been the Integrated Development Programme for the Western Isles (£20 million over 5 years), which is seeking through a comprehensive programme to stimulate the economies of the Western Isles of Scotland.

Comment The EEC Regional Directorate itself considers the non-quota section of the Regional Fund to represent a significant development in EEC policy. The Fund is likely to undergo major changes as a result. A move towards more comprehensive programmes is also leading to the consideration of more comprehensive budgets. Talks began in 1983 concerning the combination of the Regional Fund, parts of the Social Fund and the Guidance Section of the Common Agricultural Policy.

References
Central Statistical Office (1981) *Britain in the European Community*, Information Reference Pamphlet 137, HMSO, London

Pinder, D. (1983) *Regional Economic Development and Policy Theory and Practice in the European Community*, Studies in Contemporary Europe, George Allen and Unwin, London

Department of Agriculture and Fisheries for Scotland (1982) *An Integrated Development Programme for the Western Isles of Scotland*, DAFS, Scotland

The European Commission, Directorate General for Agriculture

Background The Directorate General is the body responsible for the co-ordination of the Common Agricultural Policy (which comprises 67 per cent of the EEC budget, half of which is spent on export refunds), particularly in co-ordinating the fixing of the annual target, intervention and threshold price levels of the Guarantee Section of the CAP. The Directorate General is part of the European 'civil service'.

Constitution The Directorate General oversees CAP, the principles of which are laid down in Articles 38–45 of the Treaty of Rome (1958). CAP is a common policy for agriculture which was agreed in principle in 1962, but has never been finalised.

It is the co-ordinator of annual negotiations for agricultural commodity prices, and is responsible to both the Commission and the Council of Ministers.

Workings The European Commission originates the annual price negotiations while the Directorate General sets up working parties for negotiation. These include Ministers and Ministries of Agriculture, farmers' representatives, the European Economic and Social Committee, trade unions, employers and the Agricultural Committee of the European Parliament. After these negotiations, the final approval of decisions is made by the Council of Ministers. A similar process operates for changes in structural policy.

Policy decisions take several forms:

— regulation: applicable to all member states and overriding national law;
— directive: outlines objectives binding on all member states, but permits individual methods of implementation;
— decision: specifically addressed to a government organisation or individual, and is binding on those named;
— recommendations/opinions: are not binding, but generally express the Community's view.

Guarantee or price policy is a regulation, but structural policy is a directive. The most influential directives have been those concerning farm modernisation (which outlines grant-aid available for farm capital); early retirement and farm amalgamation (designed to enlarge marginal farms by encouraging the early retirement of some farmers and the amalgamation of their farms with others); the provision of socio-economic advice; and additional grant-aid to farmers in Less Favoured Areas. This last directive allows higher rates of grant for farm capital and direct subsidies for livestock rearing, in particularly disadvantaged areas. Both elements of CAP are funded through the European Agricultural Guarantee and Guidance Fund (FEOGA). In 1981/2, Britain spent £1,039 million on CAP and £770 million was reimbursed through the FEOGA.

Comment There is common criticism by a number of authors that too much money is spent on CAP, particularly in the production of surpluses, but annual price negotiations are widely seen as a forum for 'intergovernmental politics' on a wider scale (for example, 1962 — West Germany made price concessions to France in return for support in closing the Berlin Wall; 1971 — Italy obstructed price increases until structural concessions were made).

The introduction of quotas for milk production in early 1984 seems likely to herald a period of radical change in CAP arrangements for agricultural commodities which will inevitably have major repercussions for the countryside.

References
Marsh, J.S. and Swanney, P.J. (1980) *Agriculture and the European Community*, George Allen and Unwin, London
Buckwell, A.E., Harvey, D.R., Thompson, K.J. and Parton, K.A. (1982) *The Costs of the Common Agricultural Policy*, Croom Helm, London
Harris, S., Swinbank, A. and Wilkinson, G. (1983) *The Food and Farm Policies of the European Community*, Wiley, London

The Ministry of Agriculture, Fisheries and Food

Background With a minister of Cabinet rank, the Ministry of Agriculture, Fisheries and Food is responsible for formulating and administering domestic policy for agriculture, horticulture, food and fishing. The MAFF also administers the CAP guarantee regulations and interprets the guidance directives in association with the Intervention Board for Agricultural Produce (formed in 1972, the time of entry into the EEC) and other agricultural departments (including the Welsh Office).

Constitution MAFF (headquarters at Whitehall Place, London, SW1) has 27 departments, including regional offices and divisional offices of the Agricultural Development and Advisory Service. The ADAS head office is at Great Westminster House, Horseferry Road, London, SW1.

The administrative cost of running MAFF in 1979/80 was £94 million (£60 million for ADAS). Total staff was 13,600 (ADAS approximately 4,700 but declining). In total there was one civil servant for every ten farmers, and the staffing of MAFF was just a little less than that of the European Commission as a whole.

The modern terms of reference of the Ministry derive from the 1947 Agriculture Act, which was intended to provide a stable and efficient agriculture industry, with reasonable farm incomes. The provision of cheap food became a more significant element of policy during the 1960s. EEC entry in 1972 affected only policy on price support and import quotas, as a result of the changing incidence of the burden of guaranteed prices.

There have been subsequent reaffirmations of policy. For example, the 1975 White·Paper 'Food from our Own Resources' and the 1979 White Paper 'Farming and the Nation' both proposed moves towards increasing productivity and self-sufficiency.

As well as having responsibility for the implementation of the CAP, the Ministry is also charged with control over animal and plant diseases, land drainage, food quality and public health standards in agriculture.

Workings The administration, interpretation and formulation of all policy is carried out with interested outside parties. The Ministry has particularly longstanding relationships with the National Farmers' Union and the Country Landowners' Association.

Agricultural policy is implemented through five regional MAFF offices and 30 ADAS divisional offices. Policy advice is given on agricultural elements of policy, guarantee policy, structural aspects, food quality and distribution, and farm management. Advice is also offered on socio-economic elements of policy (for example, farm tourism) but this is more active in Less Favoured Areas (see European Commission Directorate General for Agriculture).

Monitoring takes place through a confidential annual agricultural census on 4th June.

Some advice is also given on rural development (largely through the Land and Water Service of ADAS). This includes agricultural aspects of structure and local plans, agricultural land loss (with reference to agricultural land classification), agricultural building design, land drainage (consultation on development here takes place with water authorities and the Department of the Environment).

MAFF is responsible for some 36 executive and 67 advisory agencies employing some 2,500 staff at a 1979 annual cost of £47 million.

Comment British agriculture is considered by some commentators to be too expensive (its total cost, including administration, tax concessions, structural and price support, has been estimated to be as high as £5 billion per annum in 1982).

There has been criticism of MAFF having too close a relationship with the NFU and the CLA, but agriculture is widely considered politically 'safe' (usually, a majority of Cabinet ministers have farming interests).

MAFF is usually reluctant to get involved in wider issues of rural development; socio-economic advice has been relatively ineffective, but there is real concern about the threat of planning controls over agriculture.

ADAS considers itself understaffed in the face of rapid changes in agricultural technology and shifts in policy.

References
Shoard, M. (1980) *The Theft of the Countryside*, Ch. 2, Maurice Temple Smith, London
Newby, H. (1979) *Green and Pleasant Land?* Ch. 3, Hutchinson, London
Bowers, J. and Cheshire, P. (1983) *Agriculture, the Countryside and Land Use*, Methuen, London

The Department of the Environment

Background The Department of the Environment (D.o.E.) has a Minister of Cabinet rank. It was formed in 1970, to supersede, in order of formation, the 1947 Ministry of Town and Country Planning, the 1951 Ministry of Housing and Local Government, the 1964 Department of Economic Affairs (withdrawn in 1969), the 1965 Ministry of Land and Natural Resources (withdrawn in 1967) and the 1969 Department of Local Government and Regional Planning (withdrawn in 1970). It is a comprehensive environmental ministry with three main subsections: planning and local government, with an associated junior Minister; housing and construction, with an associated junior Minister; and transport. The Ministry of Transport was accorded partial independence from the D.o.E. in 1976, and has its own non-Cabinet Minister.

Constitution The D.o.E. is concerned with securing consistency and continuity in the framing of national policy with respect to the use and development of land throughout England and Wales. These responsibilities have changed little for the D.o.E. and its predecessors since the 1943 Minister of Town and Country Planning Act.

The D.o.E. is responsible for a wide range of functions including the approval of structure plans, the determination of planning appeals, regional planning co-ordination, countryside affairs, historic buildings and ancient monuments, sport and recreation, housing policy and finance, policy and finance for the water industry, the running of the Property Services Agency (responsible for all construction activities of Government departments), and major support for, and control over, local government expenditure.

Apart from the Property Services Agency, the Department is not an executive body — in general, other bodies implement Departmental policy.

Workings Headquarters: 2 Marsham Street, London, SW1P 3EP. There are 14 directorates within the D.o.E. to cover all of the main functions listed above. There are also nine regional offices and strong links with the Department of Transport, Department of Industry and local authorities.

Some 115 executive and advisory agencies of the D.o.E. (including the Countryside Commission, the Nature Conservancy Council, the Sports Council, the Development Commission and the water authorities), were reduced to 75 in 1980.

The main activities of the D.o.E. take place at four levels:

— Ministerial and Senior Officer level: formulation of policy guidelines and legislative requirements;
— Middle Administration: programme and budget inputs to the Public Expenditure Committee, annual forecasts (for example, Rate Support allocations);
— Responses to Outside Bodies: submissions by local authorities and executive agencies on financial programmes and other formal documents (for example, structure plans) requiring approval;
— Applications by Private Individuals requiring a response (planning applications, objections to schemes such as a road construction).

The D.o.E. budget 1981/2 (excluding Property Services Agency) was £2,731 million of which £2,492 million was spent on housing, £38 million was spent on planning, £47 million was spent on national heritage and £154 million was spent on administration. Total D.o.E. staff, 1982, was 8,918 which cost £86 million.

Comment There has been a criticism of the D.o.E. having a thwarted role over the environment of the countryside because it lacks control over agriculture and forestry. There is political competition between D.o.E. and MAFF in a number of instances. (For example, the incidence of the burden of compensation payments for management agreements. Here the D.o.E. through local authorities or the Nature Conservancy Council, currently incurs the cost of compensating farmers for not undertaking land-use changes in National Parks or Sites of Special Scientific Interest, where objections on environmental grounds have been made.)

There has been a great deal of bureaucratic reorganisation of environmental ministries since the war which has led to a discontinuity of policies.

It is also argued that there are too many agencies providing advice to the D.o.E. This had led to a fragmentation of policy and effort and is wasteful of resources.

References

Cloke, P. (1983) *An Introduction to Rural Settlement Planning*, Ch. 4, Methuen, London

Cullingworth, J.B. (1982) *An Introduction to Town and Country Planning*, 8th edn, Ch. 2, George Allen and Unwin, London

Bartlett School of Architecture and Planning, University College, London (1982) *Decision Making for Rural Areas, East Lindsey Study, Lincolnshire*, Appendix 4, Bartlett School, London

The Departments of Trade and Industry, Transport and Energy and the Welsh Office

Background All of these Departments are headed by a Secretary of State and all have a significant influence over rural development. There are close links with all of these Departments and the Department of the Environment.

Constitution The Department of Trade and Industry (DTI) is responsible for policy towards industry and small firms, regional industrial policy (liaising with the EEC over the Regional Development Fund) and for financial assistance to industry other than through the tax system. The Department monitors the progress of general manufacturing industries as well as public corporations. It is responsible for government research establishments and the Business Statistics Office. The Design Council and the National Research and Development Corporation also fall within its sphere.

The Department of Transport is responsible for the land surface transport industries including freight and ports, the national motorway and trunk road network, local transport policies and programmes, transport and supplementary grants, road safety, vehicle regulation and inspection, bus and road freight licensing and driver and vehicle licensing.

The Department of Energy is responsible for the development of all energy policy. It discharges governmental functions for the publicly-owned coal, gas and electricity industries and the Atomic Energy Authority. It is responsible for all energy resource development in the UK, and all international energy relations. It co-ordinates energy conservation policy.

The Welsh Office, which was set up in 1964, has a number of main areas of jurisdiction: housing, education (except universities), local government, town and country planning, new towns, health and social services, water and sewerage, transport and highways, agriculture and industry. There are over 20 advisory and executive agencies serving the Welsh Office including Development Board for Rural Wales, Welsh Development Agency and the Welsh Water Authority.

Workings Department of Trade and Industry, 124 Victoria Street, London SW1, has some 28 divisions and research units (including the Regional Development Grants Office and Small Firms Service which both have their own regional offices) as well as DTI regional offices. It is responsible for the designation and promotion of Assisted Areas (covering about 40 per cent of the working population in 1979, reduced to 25 per cent in 1982). Only Assisted Areas are eligible for EEC Regional Fund Aid. DTI activities in rural areas are independent of the Development Commission and the Council for Small Industries in Rural Areas. DTI budget in 1981/2 was £3,103 million of which £780 million was spent on regional and selective assistance and £49 million on central and miscellaneous services. In 1982, staff numbers were 8,350 with staff costs of £73 million.

The Department of Transport, 2 Marsham Street, London SW1, has some five headquarters sections, but its structural organisation, regional offices and common services are shared with the Department of the Environment. The Department budget, 1981/2, was £1,940 million of which £695 million was spent on roads. In 1982, there were 13,315 staff with staff costs of £99 million.

The Department of Energy, Thames House South, Millbank, London SW1, has 15 headquarters divisions and offices. These include a coal division which develops national policy, liaises with the National Coal Board and authorises open cast workings; an atomic energy division, to finance the Atomic Energy Authority and liaise with British Nuclear Fuels Limited; an electricity division which liaises with the Central Electricity Generating Board and develops national policy; and a gas division, to be responsible for the British Gas Corporation. The total budget of the Department of Energy (1982) was £764 million, of which £16 million was spent on administration and miscellaneous services. The 1982 staff level was 1,140, with staff costs of £13 million.

Welsh Office: London Offices, Gwydr House, Whitehall, London SW1; Cardiff Offices, Crown Buildings, Cathays Park. It has 17 Divisions or groups (including agriculture and land-use planning) to deal with its functions. There is much liaison with all government departments and ministries with equivalent functions in England. The total government expenditure for Wales (1981/2) was £1,119 million. The Welsh Office staff in 1982 was 2,300, with total staff costs of £19 million.

Comment There is a certain lack of co-ordination

between government departments in relation to policies for the countryside. The fragmented nature of the departmental organisation necessitates a large (and expensive) amount of inter-departmental liaison. For example, the DTI does not oversee the work of the Development Commission and must, therefore, liaise directly. The siting of nuclear power stations, as another instance, requires liaison between the D.o.E. and the Department of Energy.

The Welsh Office provides a more 'integrated' department to oversee a greater breadth of rural development.

References

HMSO (annually) *Britain, an Official Handbook*, Chs. 2, 8, 12, 15 (1983 edn), HMSO, London

Municipal Publications (annually) *The Municipal Yearbook*, Part 3 (1983 edn), MP Limited, London

HMSO (annually) *Supply Estimates*, Memorandum by the Chief Secretary to the Treasury, HMSO, London

HMSO (1980) *Report on Non-departmental Public Bodies*, HMSO, London, Cmnd. 7797

Section 2.2
QUANGOS AND OTHER NATIONAL BODIES

The Countryside Commission for England and Wales

Background The Countryside Commission was formed under the 1968 Countryside Act as an advisory civil service body to the Department of the Environment, replacing the National Parks Commission (created under the 1949 National Parks and Access to the Countryside Act). It was made an independent grant-in-aid body ('body corporate') under the 1981 Wildlife and Countryside Act. It is concerned to oversee landscape conservation and recreation activities over the whole of the countryside, and not just in designated areas.

Constitution The Countryside Commission (John Dower House, Crescent Place, Cheltenham, Gloucestershire) is charged with three main responsibilities: conserving the landscape beauty of the countryside; developing and improving facilities for recreation and access in the countryside; and advising government on matters of countryside interest in England and Wales. A five–year programme was produced in July, 1983 for eleven main subject areas, such as the coast, the lowlands and the uplands, in the fulfilment of these responsibilities.

There are 13 Commissioners for England and eight for Wales appointed by the Secretaries of State for the Environment and for Wales.

The Commission employed 93 staff in 1982: half in the Cheltenham headquarters (with conservation, recreation and access and communications branches), and half in regional offices in Bristol, London, Cambridge, Birmingham, Manchester, Leeds and Newcastle. The Committee for Wales is based in Newtown, Powys. The Commission has an annual grant from the Department of the Environment (£12.7 million in 1983/4).

Workings The Commission acts as a catalyst rather than an executive agency (it has no landowning interests, for example) and works through giving advice, sponsoring research and practical experimental projects and giving grant-aid (the largest allocations currently are on amenity tree-planting).

The Commission designates and advises on policies for National Parks and Areas of Outstanding Natural Beauty; it assists local authorities and private owners in improving landscape and providing for recreation; it promotes information and interpretation facilities; it advises on issues of national importance as they affect recreation and the landscape; it comments on the land use planning system as it influences the landscape of the countryside, and rural recreation opportunities; it liaises with other governmental agencies and the voluntary movement.

Comment There are some difficulties in balancing the Commission's recreation and conservation priorities. At present, clear emphasis is given to the latter.

There is increasing criticism of Commissioners' appointments being biased towards landowning interests and the farming fraternity.

The Commission has not proved to be a particularly powerful voice in rural debates, possibly due to its civil service status until 1982, and its limited statutory powers and financial resources. More recently, there has been an increase in public participation in policy formulation (notably policy for the uplands).

In looking to resolve problems of rural multiple land use, the Commission has stressed the informal management approach, which is heavily dependent on the personalities of field officers, and because of this has not always been entirely successful.

References
Countryside Commission. *Annual Reports*, Cheltenham

Countryside Commission (1982) *Prospectus: Countryside Issues and Action*, Cheltenham

Countryside Commission (1983) *Five Year Programme, 1983–1988*, Cheltenham

Cripps, J. (1979) *The Countryside Commission: Government Agency or Pressure Group?*, Town Planning Discussion Paper no. 31, Bartlett School of Architecture and Planning, University College, London

Lowe, P. (1983) 'A Question of Bias', *Town and Country Planning, 25(5)*, 132-4

The Nature Conservancy Council

Background The Nature Conservancy Council was introduced as the Nature Conservancy by Royal Charter under the 1949 National Parks and Access to the Countryside Act, and reconstituted after a number of changes in the 1960s as the Nature Conservancy Council under the 1973 Nature Conservancy Council Act. It is a statutory grant-in-aid body (via the Department of the Environment) covering Scotland as well as England and Wales.

Constitution The Nature Conservancy Council's (19/20 Belgrave Square, London SW1) main functions are: the establishment and maintenance of National Nature Reserves and Sites of Special Scientific Interest (SSSIs), advice to the government on nature conservation policy, the provision of information and advice to all interested parties especially with regard to species conservation and the safeguarding of sites, and commissioning and supporting research. Most research relating to nature conservation is actually carried out by the Institute of Terrestrial Ecology which was separated from the old Nature Conservancy in 1973.

The Council has 19 members appointed by the Secretaries of State for the Environment, Wales and Scotland. There are separate committees for England and Wales.

The Council has six Advisory Committees and four headquarters divisions: Scientific Services, Policy and Operations, Chief Land Agent and Head of Lands and Chief Scientist's Team.

There are eight regional offices in England and three in Wales.

Total NCC staff (1982) was 559. The total grant-in-aid was £10 million (1981/2), about half of which was on staff costs. The total aid for conservation purposes (1981/2) was £337,000 of which nearly £34,000 was spent on compensation payments for management agreements in SSSIs and National Nature Reserves.

Workings Research and policy are dealt with through Advisory Committees and headquarters.

Advice and information derive mainly from the regional offices. Active negotiation with local authorities commonly takes place (for example on matters of planning applications in SSSIs and National Nature Reserves, and concerning the establishment and running of local nature reserves). There is liaison with the Forestry Commission (over Forest Nature Reserves), with farmers and Ministry of Agriculture (over management agreements and other conservation measures), and with the Countryside Commission, water authorities, developers and voluntary groups, such as the county Trusts for Nature Conservation (grant-aided by the NCC and counties) and Farming and Wildlife Advisory Groups.

There are some 123 National Nature Reserves in England and Wales with a total area of 44,000 hectares. In addition, there are 3,171 SSSIs (of special interest by virtue of their flora, fauna, geological or physiographical features) approaching 800,000 hectares in extent.

Some 55 management agreements had been concluded on SSSIs and in National Nature Reserves in England and 19 in Wales by 1982 under Section 15 of the 1968 Countryside Act and Section 32 of the 1981 Wildlife and Countryside Act. The total area of these agreements was 1,560 hectares.

Comment The Council maintain that, unless the machinery for a national land use strategy is implemented soon, the present policy of isolated conservation in separate reserves will fail because of its fragmented and incremental nature.

There are problems with the payment of compensation payments for management agreements in SSSIs and National Nature Reserves, since there is insufficient money allocated to undertake agreements comprehensively or to purchase land outright.

A good collaborative relationship with the Countryside Commission over landscape conservation exists.

There is some concern on the part of the NCC over the overlapping of research functions between the NCC and the Institute of Terrestrial Ecology.

References

Nature Conservancy Council. *Annual Reports*, London
Nature Conservancy Council (1977) *A Nature Conservation Review, Towards Implementation, a Consultation Paper*, The Council, London
Sheail, J. (1976) *Nature in Trust*, Chs 6, 7 and 8, Blackie, London
Green, B. (1981) *Countryside Conservation*, Ch. 3, George Allen and Unwin, London

The Forestry Commission

Background The Forestry Commission was formed under the 1919 Forestry Act to make good timber depletion from the First World War. There have been numerous Acts since then, for example, the 1947 Forestry Act, which introduced Dedication Agreements for the private sector (that is, fiscal concessions in exchange for a management plan) and the 1951 Forestry Act, which introduced felling licences (amended in the 1967 and 1979 Forestry Acts). The main influence over current activities, however, has been the Forest Policy White Paper of 1972, which concluded that timber production alone was not economic. This has led to a diversification of the Commission's role into employment creation, amenity, conservation and access, and a temporary abandonment of the Dedication Scheme. The 1981 Forestry Act introduced the Forestry Grant Scheme for the private sector and encouraged the sale of Commission estates.

Constitution The Forestry Commission (231 Corstophine Road, Edinburgh) is responsible to the Ministry of Agriculture and the Secretary of State for Wales where appropriate (and has equivalent responsibility in Scotland and Northern Ireland). It consists of one chairman and four full-time Commissioners (a Director General, one for harvesting and marketing, one for forest and estate management and one for administration and finance). There are also five part-time Commissioners with special interests.

The Commission has two main functions. As a *forest authority* to advance knowledge and understanding of forestry, to carry out research and combat disease, to ensure the best use of timber resources and promote an efficient timber industry, to provide training and education, to administer controls and schemes to the private sector in pursuance of sound forestry and to pursue good land-use and integration with agriculture.

As a *forestry enterprise* to plant, manage and market products, to stimulate the local economy, to protect and enhance the environment, to promote recreation where appropriate, to integrate forestry and agriculture. The Commission has a target rate of return on investment of between 3 and 5 per cent.

Commission receipts (1981/2) were £116.9 million of which £57 million was government grant-aid and £39.5 million was from the sale of timber. There were 2,095 non-industrial staff and 5,450 industrial staff in 1982.

Workings As a *forestry authority*, the Commission currently provides grant aid to the private sector via the Forestry Grant Scheme, introduced in October 1981. This scheme superseded Dedication Basis III and the Small Woodlands Scheme which themselves superseded Dedication Bases I and II in 1972, when the Dedication Scheme was temporarily abandoned. The Forestry Grant Scheme is a simplified grant scheme, where differential subsidies are paid for planting and replanting, and where the primary aim is timber production. Higher rates of grant are available for broadleaves rather than conifers. A five-year Plan of Operation is required with due regard for agriculture and conservation. No felling licences are required nor Tree Preservation Orders permitted within the Plan.

The Forestry Commission has two research stations to supplement its scientific work.

As a *forestry enterprise*, the Commission currently owns some 1.2 million hectares of land, half of which is in Scotland. Some 800,000 hectares are under plantation (over half the productive forest of Britain). The Commission has eleven conservancies in Britain, each with several districts (70 in all) which are further divided into 264 Commission forests.

Comment The fact that the Commission is responsible to the Ministry of Agriculture in England has an influence over the development of forestry on agricultural land since, ultimately, MAFF has the power to sanction forestry development.

The expansion of forestry has become particularly controversial since the 1972 Treasury Cost-benefit Study and Forest Policy White Paper indicated that timber production was uneconomic. The Commission has since diversified its role, but opponents of expansion maintain that these new functions (employment, amenity, conservation and access) do not require new forestry. Critics argue that employment costs more per job than in agriculture, coniferous forests are linear and monotonous, monoculture does not encourage species diversity and new planting restricts access. There is also much dispute over forecasts of the future demand for timber.

References

Forestry Commission. *Annual Reports*, HMSO, London
Centre for Agricultural Strategy (1980) *Strategy for the U.K. Forestry Industry*, Ch. 3, CAS Report 6, University of Reading
The Ramblers' Association (1980) *Afforestation: the Case Against Expansion*, Brief for the Countryside no. 7, London
Engledow, F. and Amey, L. (1980) 'The Case for Forestry' in *Britain's Future in Farming*, Studies in Land Economy, pp. 60–72, Geographical Publications, Berkhamsted

The Development Commission

Background The Development Commission (14 Cowley Street, London SW1) is a body of eight Commissioners appointed by Royal Warrant, to report to the Department of the Environment on the disposal of the Development Fund, established by the Development and Road Improvement Funds Act of 1909 and 1910. The Development Commission (DC) was reorganised in 1974 to function as the main agency for promoting social and economic development in rural England. Under the 1983 Financial Provisions Bill, the DC was made a grant-in-aid body, responsible for its own budget.

Constitution The scope of the Development Fund has altered considerably since 1910, but is available for any scheme that may be calculated to benefit the rural economy of England (as long as no other statutory provision or help exists, such as in agriculture). Under the 1983 Bill, the Commission may acquire land by compulsory purchase and may itself give grants subject to a scheme agreed by the Department of the Environment and the Treasury. The Commission has six major areas of activity, the focus being on the economic and social health of rural communities (see below). The former is channelled through the Council for Small Industries in Rural Areas (CoSIRA) and the latter through the National Council for Voluntary Organisations and the independent Rural Community Councils. The areas of activity are:

— The creation and maintenance of employment, much of which is carried out by the Commission's agents, CoSIRA and English Estates Limited.
— The provision of housing (particularly low-cost).
— The enhancement of social and community life in rural areas, notably by the Commission's support for the Rural Department of the National Council for Voluntary Organisations and the independent Rural Community Councils.
— The supporting of rural services.
— Publicity, lobbying and information collection and dissemination. The Commission seeks to emphasise to government (central and local) the rural element of policies.
— The encouragement and sponsorship of social and economic surveys and research.

Workings In pursuit of employment creation, factory provision may be funded entirely by the Development

Commission in assisted areas in England. This is done through the agency of the English Estates Corporation (Team Valley, Gateshead, Tyne and Wear) which itself was established under the Local Employment Act of 1960, and modified under the Industrial Development Act of 1972. The Corporation is responsible to the Department of Industry whose Secretary of State appoints the Chairman and four members. Factory provision may be funded at 50 per cent in non-priority areas with a focus on Rural Development Areas (which are designated by the Development Commission itself and which are akin to Special Investment Areas which they replaced in 1984). The criteria for selecting these areas includes above average unemployment for Britain as a whole, inadequate employment opportunities, population decline, poor access to services and an ageing population. This aid is usually jointly financed with local authorities and is also carried out through English Estates.

The Commission, through CoSIRA, can also pay 35 per cent grants towards the conversion of farm buildings for craft and light industrial use in EEC-designated Less Favoured Areas.

The Commission's advances from the Development Fund in 1981/2 were £11.5 million. Of this, 51 per cent went to advance factory building, 34 per cent to CoSIRA and 12 per cent went to NCVO. Within the Commission, there was a total staff of 35 with administration and staffing costs of £556,000 (which did not come from the Development Fund).

CoSIRA (141 Castle Street, Salisbury, Wiltshire) is a limited company owned by the Development Commission, the main objective of which is to improve employment opportunities through small firms (of less than 20 skilled workers) in rural areas (towns and villages of less than 15,000 population). CoSIRA no longer builds factories itself and is restricted to building conversion, credit and advice. Most counties have a Small Industries Advisor (co-ordinated by Regional Directors instituted under the Lane Review of 1975) who draws on central specialist advice and works in collaboration with the Department of Industry's Small Firms Advisory Service. A total of 31 county offices cover 41 counties in England.

CoSIRA receives some grant-aid from the European Regional and Social Funds in addition to the £3.9 million from the Development Fund (1981/2). Staff numbers in 1982 were 305 of whom 163 worked in county offices. (Staff and administration costs, in addition to the Development Fund grant, were £2.1 million.)

Comment There are some problems with the designation of Rural Development Areas, which the Commission itself designates, since one of the criteria that should be taken into account is that unemployment should be higher than the national average. In fact, a majority of rural areas do not meet this criterion and areas that do are smaller in extent than the former Special Investment Areas. This may be leading to a reduction in areas eligible for Commission assistance at the same time as applications are being made to extend the agricultural Less Favoured Areas in England and Wales.

The Commission, like the European Regional and Social Funds, is giving increasing attention to the role of integrated rural development programmes for disadvantaged areas.

References

Development Commission and CoSIRA. *Annual Reports*, London

Whitby, M.C. and Hodge, I. (1979) *New Jobs in the Eastern Borders: an Evaluation of the Development Commission Programme*, Agricultural Adjustment Unit, Research Monograph M8, University of Newcastle-upon-Tyne

National Council for Voluntary Organisations (1982) *Country Work: A Guide to Rural Employment Initiatives*, NCVO, Rural Department, London

Clarkson, S. (1980) *Jobs in the Countryside: Some Aspects of the Work of the Rural Industries Bureau and the Council for Small Industries in Rural Areas, 1910–1979*, Occasional Paper no. 2, Department of Environmental Studies and Countryside Planning, Wye College, University of London

The English and Welsh Tourist Boards

Background Both Boards were set up in 1969, under the Development of Tourism Act (along with the British Tourist Authority (BTA) of which both Boards are members and whose objective is to promote British tourism overseas) to develop the tourism industry of England and Wales.

Constitution The English Tourist Board (4 Grosvenor Gardens, London SW1) and the Welsh Tourist Board (Brunel House, Fitzalan Road, Cardiff) are responsible respectively to the Department of Industry and the Welsh Office and are charged with developing and marketing tourism in their own countries. They aim to encourage indigenous holidays and improve tourism facilities and amenities.

They liaise with Regional Tourist Boards, the BTA, trade and training representatives and government departments on matters relating to tourism.

They develop marketing strategies for tourism (a new strategy was launched in 1982).

Workings Their Development Divisions are responsible for attracting private development and contributions from the European Regional Fund. They determine the allocation of Tourism Project Grants and grants under the Hotel Development Incentives Scheme.

Tourism Project Grants were available in assisted areas only until a Ministerial statement in August, 1982. They are now available in the whole of England and Wales. Project grant aid in England was £4.5 million to 315 projects, generating a new investment of £33 million (1982/3). Grant aid in Wales was £1.7 million to 114 projects (1981/2). Grants traditionally have been used for creating accommodation, but recently more interest has been shown in funding specific leisure attractions, such as zoos and outdoor pursuits centres.

The Hotel Development Incentives Scheme provides grants and loans for hotel development according to specific criteria. In excess of £44 million has been allocated since 1969, but a proportion of this has been repaid.

Their Research Divisions are responsible for surveys, forecasts and contracting research.

Tourist Boards generally are responsible for registering approved accommodation and giving financial assistance to local authority-run tourist information centres.

The ETB total administrative and salaries costs were £3.5 million in 1982/3, with a total staff of 183. Total grant-in-aid was £10.5 million. The WTB spent £1 million in staff and administration costs, with 76 staff (1981/2).

There are twelve Regional Tourist Boards in England, grant-aided by the ETB, local authorities and the commercial sector. There is also some generation of funds by Regional Boards (for example, the East Midlands Tourist Board's total budget in 1979/80 was £150,000, of which £56,000 came from the ETB, £40,000 came from local authorities and £40,000 came from income).

Regional Boards are responsible for the planning, development and marketing of tourism in their areas, and for advising the ETB on grant allocations. Close liaison takes place with local authorities and trade interests who sit on Regional Board executive committees.

The Wales Tourist Board has five advisory committees and three regional councils.

Comment Tourist Boards act as catalysts in developing tourism as a private sector industry, rather than direct public sector development.

There has been some criticism from the hotel trade that the grant-aid requirements of the Hotel Development Incentives Scheme are over-rigorous.

The majority of quangos with an interest in leisure (including the Sports Council, Countryside Commission and Tourist Boards) belong to a Chairman's Policy Group which acts as a forum for the discussion of new national leisure policy.

References

English and Welsh Tourist Boards. *Annual Reports*, London and Cardiff

English Tourist Board (1982) *Tourism and Leisure: the New Horizon*, ETB, London

Roper, G. and Jeffries, D. (1982) 'The English Tourist Board's Promotion "Maritime England": the Choice of Methods and Markets', Countryside Recreation Research Advisory Group Annual Report, 1982, *Countryside Recreation in the 1980s*, University of Bath, the Sports Council, London

Patmore, J.A. (1983) *Recreation and Resources*, Ch. 1, Blackwell, Oxford

The Sports Council

Background The Sports Council is an independent body established by Royal Charter in 1972 to replace the advisory Sports Council, formed in 1965. There is a separate Council for Wales, but there is close liaison between the two. Regional Councils for Sport and Recreation (RCSRs) were set up in 1975 under the White Paper 'Sport and Recreation'. Government contact with the Sports Council is through the Department of the Environment.

Constitution The Royal Charter charges the Sports Council 'to develop and improve the knowledge and practice of sport and recreation in the interests of social welfare and enjoyment, and to encourage high standards'.

The Council has overall responsibility for British sport as well as domestic affairs in England. It consists of a chairman, two vice-chairmen and 29 members appointed by the Secretary of State for the Environment. Full Council meets four times a year.

The Council has some 600 staff, with a total government grant (1983/4) of £27.03 million.

There are nine Sports Council regional offices, the directors of which are also secretaries to the RCSRs.

The nine RCSRs are autonomous, with a membership drawn from local authorities, sport, recreation and conservation organisations, farming and countryside interests, government departments and statutory agencies (for example, water authorities and tourist boards). They are serviced by Regional Council officers with assistance from the Countryside Commission.

Workings The Sports Council (16 Upper Woburn Place, London WC1) has four main national committees: Policy and Resources, National Resources, Regional Resources and Research and Information.

The main work of the Council lies in giving advice, information (including the undertaking of research) and grant-aid to the public sector, the private sector and some 60 sports associations.

The 1975 White Paper led to the development of two main schemes: Centres of Excellence and Areas of Need, to cover both ends of the sport and recreation spectrum.

A new ten-year strategy was launched in 1982, calling for £215 million over ten years to create an extra five and a half million sportspeople. The strategy has three main themes: mass participation, better sporting facilities and international sporting success. Specific attention is being given to alleviating deprivation in rural areas (as well as inner cities).

The RCSRs are non-executive forums for consultation and advice. They give grant-aid, monitor facility provision and advise the Sports Council on policy. All this is done consistent with the Regional Recreation Strategies produced under the 1975 White Paper.

Comment The majority of grant-aid has hitherto been weighted in favour of elitism, but the balance is expected to change under the ten-year strategy.

The majority of grant-aid is urban, but increasing focus is being given to countryside sports.

The Regional Councils have consolidated a trend towards 'regionalism' in resource planning.

Although the Sports Council *promotes* sport, it has a less positive role towards countryside recreation. Along with the Countryside Commission, it is only empowered to *facilitate* it. This leads to problems in the formulation of regional recreational strategies.

References
Sports Council. *Annual Reports*, London
Sports Council (1983) *Sport in the Community, the Next Ten Years*, Sports Council, London
Department of the Environment (1975) *Sport and Recreation*, White Paper, Cmnd. 6200, HMSO, London
Chairman's Policy Group (1983) *Leisure Policy for the Future*, Sports Council, London

The Development Board for Rural Wales and the Welsh Development Agency

Background These are two of the principal executive agencies of the Welsh Office set up in the mid 1970s to co-ordinate economic and social development in Wales.

Constitution The Development Board for Rural Wales (DBRW) was established by the Secretary of State for Wales under the Development of Rural Wales Act, 1976, to prepare and carry out measures for the social and economic development of Mid-Wales (40 per cent of the land area of Wales, but only 7 per cent of the population).

The Welsh Development Agency (WDA) was established under the Welsh Development Agency Act of 1975, to regenerate the economy, improve the environment and promote industrial efficiency and international competitiveness throughout all of Wales. It has an executive membership of ten, including the Chief Executive.

Workings DBRW (Ladywell House, Newtown, Powys) is concerned to promote economic and social development, primarily concentrated on designated growth towns (in an area where 60 per cent of the population live in isolated farms and small hamlets), although any enterprise in Mid-Wales is considered for assistance. The 1981 Census showed the first clear increase in the Mid-Wales population for 100 years. Part of Mid-Wales lost its assisted area status in 1982, hampering the work of the Board. There is very close liaison with the three county councils and five district councils in the area.

The DBRW had a budget of £6.6 million (plus £1.8 million in housing subsidies) in 1981/2. The Board employed 96 permanent staff with an expenditure of £1.2 million on wages and administration in 1982. The main areas of grant assistance were: industrial construction (£3.35 million): commerce (£629,000); housing (£1.38 million); social and economic grants, including amenity and leisure (£419,000). In addition to this budget, the repayment of loan charges was £4.16 million.

The WDA (Treforest Industrial Estate, Pontypridd, Glamorgan) builds factories and industrial estates, provides investment capital (partly through its Small Business Unit), promotes growth and reclaims derelict land (with local authorities). It is the biggest industrial landlord in Wales and (with its predecessors) provides a third of all manufacturing jobs in Wales.

The gross expenditure of the WDA (1982/3), was £75 million. (The EEC Social Fund provided £0.2 million and the Regional Fund provided £0.3 million.) The number of staff in 1982 was 586.

Main environmental improvements carried out by the WDA include £10.4 million to local authorities for derelict land improvement (grants up to 100 per cent are available to reinstate land which has been subsequently re-used, for example, in agriculture or as Country Parks, chiefly in South Wales). The 1982 Derelict Land Act allows grants to the private sector. Some building improvements and environmental works (with the Prince of Wales Committee) have also been undertaken.

Comment There is criticism of both agencies having a bias towards project-specific development rather than wider community programmes as in the non-quota section of the European Regional Development Fund. The DBRW, however, does spend money on social and community development and has a broad remit for grant-aid in the selected growth areas.

The DBRW particularly represents a very small financial input into rural Wales compared with agricultural support, with little control over the agriculture sector, the main cause of rural depopulation.

These types of agency are considered to offer considerable potential for rural development if their remit is wide enough. Similar boards to the DBRW were proposed in England by the short-lived Ministry of Land and Natural Resources (1965–7) under the 1967 Agriculture Act, but only one came into being.

References
DBRW and WDA. *Annual Reports*
Tranter, R.B. (ed.) (1978) *The Future of Upland Britain*, CAS Paper no. 2, Papers 24, 45, and 50, University of Reading, Centre for Agricultural Strategy
Brody, M. (1980) 'Rural Regeneration: a Note on the Mid-Wales Case', *Cambria, 7(i)*, 79–85

The Historic Buildings Councils for England and Wales

Background Both Councils were set up under the Historic Buildings and Ancient Monuments Act of 1953, taking their present terms of reference from Orders from the Secretaries of State for the Environment and for Wales in 1970, to whom the English and Welsh Councils respectively are responsible. The English Council was amalgamated in 1984, with the Ancient Monuments Board to create a new grant-in-aid Commission to be responsible for all aspects of conservation of historic buildings and ancient monuments.

Constitution The Councils are to advise the Secretaries of State for the Environment and for Wales about the making of grants and loans for the repair and maintenance of historic buildings and adjoining lands. Also advice is to be given about the acquisition of such buildings and on the enhancement of conservation areas. Recommendations are made for the listing of buildings and new uses for old buildings.

Salient Acts determining these terms of reference are the 1953 Act, the Civic Amenities Act, 1967, the Town and Country Amenities Act, 1974, the Local Government Planning and Land Act, 1980.

There is one Chairman and 20 members of the Council for England and one Chairman and six members for the Council of Wales.

Workings The Councils for England (25 Savile Row, London W1) and for Wales (Welsh Office, Cathays Park, Cardiff) give advice on historic houses, industrial buildings, farm buildings and both churches in use and redundant churches. In addition, they both have a role to play in designated conservation areas, both urban and rural.

The Councils assist in the development of building conservation policy in conjunction with the Historic Buildings Division of the Department of the Environment and formulate criteria for the listing of buildings (there are currently 325,000 listed buildings in Britain). The Councils advise the Treasury on the designation of historic buildings and in 1984 compiled directories on historic gardens (for the guidance of traffic engineers and local authorities) and historic house contents.

Grants to historic buildings in England (1981/2) were £8.3 million, and to conservation areas in England (1981/2) were £3.4 million.

Comment There is some criticism that the Commission introduced in 1984 is indicative of the government seeking to relinquish its responsibility for heritage work or attempting to reduce financial support in this area. To counter this, the Department of the Environment stress the amount of duplication that there was between the Ancient Monuments Board and the Historic Buildings Council that is now avoided.

The former Historic Buildings Council for England was keen that the proposed new Commission should have charitable status to enjoy tax advantages in relation to private donations and should have the power to set up a trading company.

Grant-aid in the countryside is mainly for historic buildings and churches, rather than conservation areas.

References

Historic Buildings Councils for England and Wales. *Annual Reports*, London and Cardiff

Gilg, A. (ed.) (1983) *Countryside Planning Yearbook*, Literature Review on Conservation, Geo Books, Norwich

Department of the Environment (1982) *Organisation of Ancient Monuments and Historic Buildings in England: The Way Forward*, HMSO, London

Significant Landowning Interests

Background Just over 1 per cent of the adult population owns almost 70 per cent of land in Britain. Central Government owns over 400,000 hectares of farmland (chiefly the Ministry of Defence), and over 1,200,000 hectares of forest and woodland (Forestry Commission). Sixty-four per cent of agricultural land is owner occupied, the remainder is tenanted. Traditional institutions own 9 per cent of agricultural land and financial institutions over 1 per cent. Britain is one of the few countries in the world not to have an open system of land registration.

Institutions and Workings *The Royal Family* has several significant estates including Balmoral, 34,680 hectares; Sandringham, 8,000 hectares (including six villages).

The Duchy of Cornwall (10 Buckingham Gate, London SW1), was instituted in 1337 by Edward III and is the personal property of the male heir to the throne. The estates are not bounded by planning laws. Income from the estate is approximately £500,000 a year, tax free. Prior to July, 1981 (the marriage of the Prince of Wales), 50 per cent of this income went to the Treasury. This is now 25 per cent. Recently there has been a more commercial approach to management and increases in rents.

The Crown Estate Commissioners (13/15 Carlton House Terrace, London SW1). Land revenues of the Crown have been collected on public account since 1760, when George III surrendered them for a fixed annual payment or Civil List. In the year to April 1982 income to the Civil List was £28 million and expenditure was £14 million. Within the estate there is ownership of approximately 140,000 hectares of farm and forest land, but the main income comes from Central London assets. There are eight Commissioners who are active on the agricultural land market.

Church Commissioners for England (1 Millbank, Westminster, London SW1). The Commission was established in April, 1948 to improve stipends, housing and pensions for clergy and their wives through the management of endowments. There are 95 Commissioners. The Commission owns 69,200 hectares of agricultural and woodland, the market value of which was £207 million in 1982. The annual income from rural land (1982) was approximately £7 million (but £29 million from urban property). There is frequent buying and selling of agricultural land.

The Oxford and Cambridge Colleges own 64,000 hectares of farmland but this amount is diminishing. Two-thirds of this land is owned by Oxford. Both universities gain tax privileges from charitable status. Other educational institutions own about 32,000 hectares together.

The Aristocracy. Twenty-six Dukes own over 400,000 hectares. (Duke of Northumberland, 36,314 hectares, Earl of Lonsdale, 27,600 hectares, Duke of Devonshire, 24,920 hectares.) This is a declining sector of ownership.

Financial Institutions. Insurance companies and pension funds own in excess of 260,000 hectares of farmland (1982). They purchase mainly high quality land. Purchases by financial institutions are rarely less than half of all farmland sales each month. The Northfield Report estimates that institutions will own 11 per cent of all agricultural land by 2020.

Comment Traditional landownership is in decline and institutional landownership is on the increase, but less than 2 per cent of farmland changes hands every year, so ownership patterns will be slow to change.

References

Harrison, A., Tranter, R.B. and Gibbs, R.S. (1977) *Landownership by Public and Semi-public Institutions in the United Kingdom*, Centre for Agricultural Strategy, University of Reading, Paper no. 3

HMSO (1979) *Report of the Committee of Inquiry into the Acquisition and Occupancy of Agricultural Land* (the Northfield Report), Cmnd. 7599, London

Munton, R. (1980) 'The Northfield Report, A Comment' in Gilg, A. (ed.) *Countryside Planning Yearbook* Geo Books, Norwich

Norton-Taylor, R. (1982) *Whose Land is it Anyway?* Turnstone Press, Wellingborough

The Water Sector

Background The organisation of the water sector has undergone a number of significant changes since the 1944 Water Supplies and Sewerage Act. There were major organisational changes resulting from the 1963 Water Resources Act and the sector's current structure derives from the 1973 Water Act. Each change has led to a reduction in the number of water agencies, with increased autonomy for regional water authorities. The main impacts on the countryside are the continuing development of storage reservoirs in upland areas and the effective limitations on building in rural areas where main sewerage works are considered too expensive.

Constitution Under the 1973 Act, the National Water Council (1 Queen Anne's Gate, London SW1), was to advise the Secretaries of State for the Environment and Wales and the Minister of Agriculture on national water policy and on the efficient performance of the nine regional water authorities and the Welsh Water Authority. The Council was to act as co-ordinator, consultant and advisor. The National Water Council was disbanded in September 1983 and its functions were taken over by the Water Authorities Association.

Central policy covers conservation, the development of water resources, distribution, sewerage, pollution, navigation and recreation.

The principal water authority responsibilities are the management of water services, water distribution, pollution, sewerage, sea defences, recreation and inland fisheries.

The total staff of the water industry was approximately 60,000 in 1982. There are current proposals to reduce water authority membership commensurate with the Welsh Water Authority reductions in 1982 (from 15 to nine members).

There are four supporting national water research centres.

Workings Water authorities have almost complete control over the industry. The exceptions are the Ministry of Agriculture which has control over land drainage policy and fisheries; 29 statutory private water companies which account for about 25 per cent of the total supplies and work under licence to water authorities; and district councils which act as agents for public sewerage works.

Authorities interface with the countryside through landownership; liaison with Countryside Commission, Nature Conservancy Council and local authorities about operations; and as pollution 'watchdogs' under the 1974 Control of Pollution Act.

Of the water abstracted (32,000 megalitres/day) 50 per cent goes to public supply, 33 per cent goes to electricity generation, 15 per cent goes to industry, and 2 per cent goes to agriculture.

The authorities' estimated revenue in 1982/3 was £2,080 million, which covers all capital investment and revenue expenditure.

Comment The water sector is coming under increasing criticism for adopting an 'engineering' approach to resource development (concentrating on the supply of resources rather than demand). There is a preoccupation with increasing supply, especially with new reservoirs, at the expense of rural land and the rural environment. Little thought is given to control of demand and, therefore, reductions in supply requirements. Was Kielder Reservoir really needed at a cost of £170 million and a loss of more than 1,000 hectares of rural land?

There has been some control over demand by optional metering in all authorities since April, 1982. Also the Drought Act, 1976, gives powers to authorities to restrict consumption in times of severe water shortage.

There is some criticism of larger authorities being not sufficiently publicly accountable and too remote from their consumers.

References

Herrington, P. (1979) *Nor any Drop to Drink?*, Occasional Paper Series, Economics Association, London

Jackson, I.C. and Bird, P.A. (1976) 'Water Supply, the Transformation of an Industry', *Three Banks Review*, March, no. 73

Okun, D.A. (1977) *The Regionalisation of Water Management*, Applied Science Publishers, Barking

Parker, O.J. and Penning-Rowsell, E.C. (1981) *Water Planning in Britain*, George Allen and Unwin, London

Pearce, F. (1982) *Watershed*, Junction Books, London

The Energy Sector

Background The executive functions of the Department of Energy (which is responsible for all policy formulation for energy resource development) are carried out chiefly by four publicly owned agencies: the Central Electricity

Generating Board (CEGB), the British Gas Corporation (BGC), the National Coal Board (NCB) and the Atomic Energy Authority (UKAEA). All have a significant environmental impact on the countryside and all have stated policies for environmental improvement. The 1983 Energy Act and the Oil and Gas (Enterprise) Act, 1982 allow for some privatisation of the energy sector.

Constitution The National Coal Board (Hobart House, Grosvenor Place, London SW1) was constituted in 1946 under the Coal Industry Nationalisation Act. Its powers now derive from all Coal Industry Acts from 1946. There are eight to 14 members, appointed by the Secretary of State for Energy.

The Central Electricity Generating Board (Sudbury House, 15 Newgate Street, London EC1) was constituted under the Electricity Act, 1957. There are seven to nine members (appointed by the Secretary of State), and twelve area boards with five to seven members each.

The British Gas Corporation (59 Bryanston Street, Marble Arch, London W1) superseded the Gas Council (constituted under the 1972 Gas Act) in 1973. It has 10 to 20 members (appointed by the Secretary of State). Area gas boards were disbanded in 1973.

The United Kingdom Atomic Energy Authority (11 Charles II Street, London SW1) was constituted under the Atomic Energy Act, 1954 (amended 1959, 1965 and 1971). It has seven to 15 members (appointed by Secretary of State).

Workings The National Coal Board has an almost complete monopoly over extraction, although some licences are issued for open-cast sites (for example, in the Forest of Dean). Its terms of reference are to secure the efficient development of the industry in the public interest and it executes the day-to-day management of the industry. Its turnover in 1981/2 was £4,727 million (operating loss, £48.2 million, government grants, £575 million). Total manpower was 212,843 (1982). Much work has been carried out on environmental restoration of coal workings in the countryside, especially back to agriculture, forestry and recreation. NCB has an Environmental Planning Committee and has won several major environmental awards.

The CEGB is concerned to maintain an efficient electricity industry, to generate and acquire supplies of electricity to provide bulk supplies to five Area Boards. Area Boards are responsible for distribution but may also acquire and generate electricity themselves. Its trading profit in 1982/3 was £705 million (total income £7,039 million). Total manpower (1983) was 52,828 (total salaries £689 million). The Board has an environmental section and a planning department. Most generating developments are landscaped for amenity purposes. There are several CEGB-owned nature trails, reserves and study centres as well as some recreational access. In addition, much work is undertaken on environmental pol-

lution and research is carried out into more environmentally sensitive forms of electricity generation. Despite a large operating profit, little attempt is made to reduce the environmental impact of pylons in the countryside, as part of the national grid. Such work is resisted on cost grounds.

The British Gas Corporation has the responsibility to maintain an efficient gas industry and satisfy all reasonable demands; to explore for natural gas and oil; to manufacture and distribute gas and sell gas by-products; to manufacture and sell gas fittings. Its turnover (1982/3) was £5,958 million (profit £663 million). Total staff in 1982 was 116,000. The Corporation has an Environmental Planning Department concerned with both pollution and landscape restoration from both distribution and exploration works.

The UKAEA has the responsibility to produce, use and dispose of nuclear energy and carry out research; to dispose of radioactive substances; to provide education on nuclear science. Expenditure in 1981/2 was £382.7 million. Manpower in 1982 was 14,350. Main environmental efforts are concerned with the safety of radioactive waste (£45 million spent in 1982). Much research in this area is financed by British Nuclear Fuels Limited and the Department of the Environment.

Comment The 'Coal and the Environment' report (Flowers Commission, 1981) suggests that much more money is required for environmental improvements of coal after-use.

Generally there is an allocation of resources and manpower towards the protection of the rural environment by the energy sector, and there is much active restoration work. However the NCB and the CEGB in particular still have a significant detrimental environmental impact on the countryside.

Nuclear power remains the most controversial energy source environmentally, but research into more environmentally sensitive forms of energy is increasing, particularly by the CEGB.

References

Clark, A.J. (1980) *Electricity Supply and the Environment*, CEGB, Publication G971, London

Down, C.G. and Stocks, J. (1977) *The Environmental Impact of Mining*, Applied Science Publishers, Barking

NCB, BGC, CEGB and UKAEA *Annual Reports*

National Coal Board (1983) *New Land from Old*, NCB, London

Swann, D.J. and Morris, R.P. (1980) *Keep it Clean, Keep it Green*, Research Division, British Gas Corporation, London

Wallace, D. (1976) *Energy We Can Live With*, Rodale Press Inc., Erasmus, Pennsylvania

Section 2.3
THE LOCAL AUTHORITY SECTOR

County Councils

Background County Councils with jurisdiction over rural areas (non-metropolitan counties) were constituted under the Local Government Act of 1972 and introduced in April 1974. The 39 non-metropolitan counties of England are, with five exceptions, virtually the same as the counties they replaced. In Wales, Glamorgan was divided into three non-metropolitan counties and the remaining twelve were merged into a further five non-metropolitan counties. The metropolitan counties contain some rural areas.

Constitution County Councils consist of a chairman and councillors. Each county has electoral divisions which, since 1977, return one councillor elected for a term of four years. Councillors are advised by officers in a number of departments.

Non-metropolitan counties have a number of functions, some of which are concurrent (c) with their constituent non-metropolitan districts:

- social services;
- education — schools, colleges etc., libraries, museums and galleries (c);
- housing and town development (c);
- town and country planning — structure plans, local plans (in special cases, for example, Cornwall's Countryside Local Plan), some development control (for example, minerals), land acquisition and disposal, derelict land clearance (c), National Parks (through National Park authorities), country parks (c), footpaths and bridleways (c), caravan sites (c), the provision of gypsy sites, smallholdings;
- highways — transport planning, public transport co-ordination, highways, traffic, road safety;
- consumer protection;
- other environmental services — land drainage, refuse disposal;
- police and fire;
- recreation and tourism (c);
- licensing and registration.

Sections 101–2 of the 1972 Act can arrange for district councils to take over some of these functions on an agency basis.

County Councils ultimately take their policy directives from the Department of the Environment, but are independent agencies. The largest central government control comes through the capital and revenue budgets of counties, which are strongly influenced by rate support grant allocations. Thus central government can control County Council expenditure to a significant extent.

Workings The Bains Report (1972) recommended a formula for County Council management structures: a chief executive with a management team of departmental directors to ensure policy collaboration. Such corporate management has been less successful in some authorities than others.

Decision-making is based on a committee system of the full council of members. Such committees have grown in both size and number since 1972 and usually reflect the services for which the county is responsible, and the departmental structure of the county.

Under the 1972 Act a council may delegate its powers to committees (made up of both members and officers), sub-committees or even individual officers. Sub-committees and committees are generally open to the public.

The Association of County Councils (66a Eaton Square, London SW1) was formed in 1973 to act as a mouthpiece for County Councils in England and Wales. The Welsh Counties Committee also performs a similar function.

Comment A total of 65 per cent of non-metropolitan county expenditure is on education. This gives counties an important influence over rural settlement patterns, particularly through the maintenance and closure of rural primary schools.

The production of annual transport policies and programmes (TPPs) also provides a strong determinant of the distribution of the rural population.

There has been some criticism by a number of authors that the political structure of the shire counties is dominated by either farmers and landowners, or more wealthy in-migrants, or both. This composition of membership, it is argued, serves to reinforce a 'no development' ethic in the countryside at the expense of the rural poor.

County planning authorities have a less clearly defined role in the post-structure plan period, since much of the implementation of these strategic documents falls to the district authorities and the local plan process.

References

County Councils. *Annual Reports and Accounts*

Richards, P.G. (1983) *The Local Government System,* The New Local Government System No. 5, George Allen and Unwin, London

Cloke, P.J. (1983) *An Introduction to Rural Settlement Planning,* Ch. 8, Methuen, London

Report of the Bains Committee (1972) *The New Local Authorities: Management and Structure,* HMSO, London

District Councils

Background District Councils with jurisdiction over rural areas (non-metropolitan districts) were constituted under the Local Government Act of 1972 and introduced in April, 1974. The boundaries of the 37 Welsh districts were determined under the Act, but the boundaries of the 296 districts of England were proposed by the first report of the Local Government Boundary Commission, and adopted through Parliamentary Orders.

Constitution District Councils consist of a chairman and councillors. These may be elected either once every four years (182 English districts and 30 in Wales) or in rotation every year, except when there are County Council elections (termed 'by thirds' — 114 English districts and seven in Wales).

Non-metropolitan districts have a number of functions, some of which are concurrent (c) with parent County Councils:

- education — museums and art galleries (c);
- housing and town development (c);
- town and country planning — local plans (most), development control (most), land acquisition and disposal, derelict land clearance (c), country parks (c), footpaths and bridleways, caravan sites (c), gipsy sites (management), allotments;
- highways;
- environmental health;
- other environmental services — sewers, refuse collection, litter, building regulations, street cleaning, cemeteries, markets;
- recreation and tourism — swimming baths (c), open spaces (c);
- licensing and regulation functions.

Workings The committee and management structures of districts are similar to those of County Councils.

Districts are not subordinate nor answerable to counties, except where acting as an agent.

The Association of District Councils (9 Buckingham Gate, London SW1) comprises all of the non-metropolitan districts in England and Wales and was formed to further the interests of the districts and the local authority service in general. The Council for the Principality also performs a similar function in Wales.

Comment The 1968 Transport Act allows districts to subsidise rural transport services, thus having an impact on the rural population.

Local Government reorganisation has brought districts into conflict with counties in a number of instances, particularly over the interpretation of structure plans in the formulation of local plans.

References

Wright, S. (1982) *Parish to Whitehall: Administrative Structure and Perceptions of Community in Rural Areas,* Gloucestershire Papers in Local and Rural Planning, Issue no. 16

Stanyer, J. (1976) *Understanding Local Government,* Fontana Books, London

Poole, K.P. (1978) *Local Government Services in England and Wales,* George Allen and Unwin, London

Parish and Town Councils

Background Parish and town councils were introduced in 1974 under the 1972 Local Government Act. Collectively they are termed local councils (where county and district councils are termed local authorities). In Wales they are known as community councils. Parish councils *must* be established by district councils where parishes have over 200 electors, and *may* be established with less than 200 electors.

Constitution Councils consist of elected members although sub-committees and advisory committees may contain non-elected members (two-thirds of these committees must be elected members, however, for them to have executive functions). Councils must hold an annual general meeting and meet at least three times a year.

Parish and town councils have jurisdiction over the following: footway lighting, footpaths, cemeteries, allotments, village greens, parish halls, public seats, commons, recreation, playing fields, litter control, roadside verges, war memorials, swimming baths, off-street car parks, byelaws, public walks, pleasure boats, public shelters, public clocks, arts and crafts, the encouragement of tourism, the provision of mortuaries, the clearing of drainage of ponds, public conveniences, washhouses and launderettes.

Under the 1972 Act parish councils for the first time gained the right to be notified of planning applications.

Parish councils have rights of appointment to the management of state primary schools.

Workings Because parish councils have no officers apart, usually, from a part-time or full-time clerk, much use is made of specialist advice (for example, legal and accounting services) of the county associations of parish and town councils (all counties) and the National Association of Local Councils (100 Great Russell Street, London WC13 3LD) which has in excess of 7,000 members.

Parish councils are allowed a 'free' 2p precepted rate to spend on anything to benefit the inhabitants that is not covered by the statutory responsibilities of the parish. This might include, for example, a parish newsletter, running a minibus, provision of a public telephone, or surveys. This 'free' 2p rate is also available to county and district councils, but is less used by them.

Money may be obtained for statutory parish use from a number of sources, in addition to the 2p rate: rate precepts via the district councils, expenditure under the Allotments Act of 1908, fees for district council agency work, grants from county councils, lotteries, subscriptions and by borrowing. Parish councils may also buy and sell land.

Parish councils have an important consultative role to play with both official bodies and the voluntary sector.

Comment There is a trend for more and more decisions to be taken at a local council level, since they are the tier of local government that interfaces with the local population, and districts have become more remote since the Local Government Act of 1972.

A nationwide review of parish boundaries is being undertaken currently by district councils, under the auspices of the Local Government Boundary Commission, to report in 1984.

A number of parish councils are increasingly using the 2p rate to initiate employment creating measures.

References

Arnold-Baker, C. (1981) *Local Council Administration,* Wilson and Sons, Kendal

Hargreaves, D. (1979) *The Parish Councillors Handbook,* The Municipal Group Limited, London

National Council for Voluntary Organisations (1982) *Country Work: A Guide to Rural Employment Initiatives,* Ch. 5, NCVO Rural Department, London

Prophet, J. (1979) *The Law of Local Councils,* Shaw and Sons, London

National Park Authorities

Background National Parks in England and Wales were conceived and defined by the 1945 Dower Report, selected by the Hobhouse Report of 1947, and established under the 1949 National Parks and Access to the Countryside Act. They were defined by Dower to be extensive areas of beautiful and relatively wild country for landscape and nature conservation and access to open countryside. Ten National Parks were designated between 1951 and 1957: Brecon Beacons, Dartmoor, Exmoor, Lake District, Northumberland, North York Moors, Peak District, Pembrokeshire Coast, Snowdonia and Yorkshire Dales. Some changes concerning Parks were introduced under the 1968 Countryside Act, but their present terms of reference are taken from the 1972 Local Government Act, enacted in April, 1974.

Constitution The broad terms of reference under the 1949 Act were to preserve and enhance the natural beauty of the Parks, and to promote their enjoyment by the public, executing both with due regard to the needs of agriculture and forestry.

Prior to 1974, National Park Authorities were disparate in their organisation. Since 1974 this has been more standardised. Each Park is now administered by an independent single executive committee or board, a maximum of two-thirds of whose members are drawn from local councils, the rest being nominated by the Secretaries of State for the Environment and for Wales, where appropriate. Each Park must have a National Park Officer. Membership varies between 18 (Pembrokeshire Coast) and 33 (Peak District). Two authorities are boards (Lake District and Peak District), four are single county committees (Dartmoor, Northumberland, Pembrokeshire Coast and Snowdonia) and the rest have multi-county committees.

Exchequer grants cover the cost of administration and capital expenditure (prior to 1974, they only covered capital, and administrative costs were borne by the local rates) and amounted to £6.69 million in 1982/3 for all ten Parks.

Workings Authorities have two basic roles — to act as a local planning authority and as a Park Authority. In pursuit of the former, the Lake District and Peak District, as boards, are structure plan authorities and exercise the planning and countryside functions of both county and district councils. The remainder, as committees, have development control and countryside management functions and, usually, delegated functions from counties for the preparation of local plans. They also have responsibilities for the conservation of areas of archaeological and historical interest, the making of tree preservation orders, advertisement control and footpath maintenance.

As a Park Authority, they must manage the Park for National Park purposes. This includes the preparation of a National Park Management Plan (the majority of which were submitted to the Secretaries of State in 1977), the negotiation of access agreements and orders (1968 Countryside Act) and of management agreements (1971 Town and Country Planning Act and 1981 Wildlife and Countryside Act). They can buy land for both access and conservation purposes, and can undertake a number of improvement works and create bye-laws. Landowners must give twelve months notification to authorities of the intention to convert moor and heathland. Because of limited finance and staff, much of this Park Authority function is carried out through negotiation and persuasion.

The Authorities have no jurisdiction over highways or traffic management.

Comment There is criticism by a number of authors that authority membership has been biased towards the farming community, particularly since the Conservatives took office in 1979. Members who are 'experienced in farming and related activities' have risen by 50 per cent nationally since 1979.

Several proposals for new National Parks have been unsuccessful. Norfolk Broads and South Downs (both originally suggested by Hobhouse) have recently been revived, but are considered to have too much recreation pressure. The Cambrian National Park in Mid-Wales was successfully opposed by local farming interests.

Authorities now place a higher priority on landscape conservation than recreational access in areas of conflict between the two, in line with the 1974 Sandford Report recommendations (which also suggested improvements in landscape design, access and wardening as well as wider controls over agriculture and forestry).

National Parks often have to accede to developments deemed to be of national significance, but which are nevertheless damaging to the environment (for example, limestone and fluorspar mining in the Peak District, potash in the North Yorkshire Moors, A66 improvements in the Lake District).

References

National Park Authorities (Mainly 1977) *National Park Plans*, for the 10 Authorities

Brotherton, I. (1981) *Conflict, Consensus, Concern and the Administration of Britain's National Parks*, Department of Landscape Architecture, Sheffield University

Department of the Environment (1974) *Report of the National Park Policies Review Committee* (Chairman, Lord Sandford), HMSO, London

McEwen, A. and McEwen, M. (1982) *National Parks, Conservation or Cosmetics?*, George Allen and Unwin, London

PART 3
Private Groups

HAROLD BRIDGES LIBRARY
S. MARTIN'S COLLEGE
LANCASTER

Section 3.1
ECONOMIC

The Agricultural and Allied Workers' National Trade Group of the Transport and General Workers' Union (Formerly the National Union of Agricultural and Allied Workers) 1907

Background The trade union representing the interests of agricultural workers, as well as other rural manual workers, was formed in East Anglia where it retains its strongest base.

Its chief concerns are to improve the wages and working conditions of agricultural workers and to promote their interests in policy-making. It has around 90,000 members organised in some 3,000 local branches and District Offices.

In 1982, its dwindling membership and dire financial position led it to amalgamate with the Transport and General Workers' Union which already had 11,000 farm workers in membership.

Workings To its members, it offers a number of services including welfare advice, accident and sickness benefits, legal aid, advice on accommodation and political representation.

Originally radical and militant, with a strong commitment to land nationalisation and a readiness to instigate strike action, it has become ever more pragmatic, confining itself largely to negotiations over agricultural wages and conditions locally and nationally.

It has sought a political voice through its affiliation to the Labour Party, its Parliamentary Committee, its one sponsored MP and its involvement in the wider trade union movement. One of the political fruits of these efforts was the Rent (Agriculture) Act, 1976, which introduced certain safeguards for tenants of tied cottages. The Union had been pressing this issue since its earliest days.

Comment Despite the Union's efforts, the agricultural worker is still one of the lowest paid and poorly accommodated workers in the country, and farming is one of the most dangerous occupations. The Union's gains have, therefore, been limited more to specific cases than to any general improvement.

Its weakness has been diagnosed in structural and ideo-logical terms. A highly scattered and fragmented workforce leads to a weak market situation and grave difficulties of organisation. It has only ever been able to recruit a minority of farm workers, thus precluding strike action. Support for the Union and a more demonstrative stance is undermined by the conservatism of many farm workers, reinforced by their close personal ties with their employers, and by the ability of many of them to agree a better wage deal with 'the gaffer' than the Union can achieve through national negotiations. Thus it is trapped in a vicious circle — its lack of power is based ultimately on a low level of organisation which in turn stems partly from its weakness in wage bargaining.

The Union has also been ambivalent about its overall political strategy, torn between its ideological commitment to the urban-oriented Labour Movement and its community of interest with farmers in the prosperity of the agricultural sector. The consequence is that it has become neither a partner with the National Farmers' Union in agricultural policy-making nor mounted an effective challenge to the NFU's political hegemony.

A very hierarchical body with a highly centralised decision-making structure, it has very little membership participation. Its affiliation to the TGWU is likely to increase the distance between individual farm workers and Union decision-making.

Address
308 Gray's Inn Road,
London WC1X 8DS

References
The Landworker, the Unions's monthly newspaper
Newby, H. (1977) *The Deferential Worker*, Penguin Books, Harmondsworth
Winyard, S. (1984) ''The Corporate Estate' in M.L. Harrison (ed.), *Corporatism and the Welfare State*, Gower, Farnborough, pp. 111–21

The Country Landowners' Association 1907

Background The national organisation representing the interests of rural landowners. Formed in 1907 as the Landholders' Central Association it became the Central

Landowners' Association in 1918, and the Country Landowners' Association in 1949.

As a promotional and advisory body for landowning interests, it has sought firstly to ensure the continuation and profitability of private landownership; and secondly to protect and conserve the countryside, both in landscape and social terms.

Throughout its history, it has sought to reconcile conservation and agricultural interests through sympathetic land management. It was a founder member of the Council for the Protection of Rural England and the Farming and Wildlife Advisory Group.

On matters of agricultural policy it is overshadowed by the NFU, whose lead it usually follows. There is very close co-operation between the two organisations.

Its 50,000 members together own the bulk of land in England and Wales. They are organised into 47 County Branches. Although 50 per cent of its members own less than 40 hectares and only 20 per cent more than 100 hectares, it is dominated by big landowners.

Workings It has extensive contacts with Parliament and Whitehall. It is well represented in the House of Lords and among the political establishment of many rural counties. In addition, it has co-operative links with a number of statutory bodies, including the Countryside Commission, the Nature Conservancy Council, the Forestry Commission and Regional Water Authorities.

It runs a comprehensive advisory service for its members, dealing with all aspects of landownership.

Comment A very influential group, particularly in its behind-the-scenes contacts with government. Although it avoids any overt party political affiliation, its obvious concern is with the profitability of landownership and the political roles of many of its leading members link it ideologically and practically with the Conservative Party.

It promotes the image of the landowner as the custodian of the landscape. It has always been interested in rural conservation and has ensured the representation of landowning interests in conservation debates. It has staunchly opposed any conservation measures which might limit the freedom of the individual landowner.

Address
16 Belgrave Square,
London SW1X 8PQ

References
Cox, G. and Lowe, P. (1984) 'Agricultural Politics and the Wildlife and Countryside Act' in Bradley, T. and Lowe, P. (eds), *Locality and Rurality: Economy and Society in Rural Regions*, Geo Books, Norwich

Newby, H. *et al.* (1978) *Property, Paternalism and Power*, Hutchinson, London

Self, P. and Storing, H. (1962) *The State and the Farmer*, George Allen and Unwin, London

Country Landowner, The monthly magazine of the CLA

Forestry Interests in the Countryside: The Economic Forestry Group PLC, The Timber Growers United Kingdom

The Economic Forestry Group PLC 1958
A commercial association of woodland owners and managers, forest economists and representatives of the timber industry, whose aim is to encourage all aspects of commercial forestry. Its main role is managing woodland on behalf of investment companies and other clients seeking the tax advantages of forestry investment.

A public company with part or full ownership of twelve operating companies and a close involvement in a number of other commercial enterprises, it recorded an annual turnover of £27 million in 1982.

Its activities include forestry consultancy, management, ownership, landscaping, investment and marketing. It holds and manages 98,000 hectares of forest in mainland Britain and is increasingly investing in overseas plantations, wood harvesting and timber processing.

It is employed on an advisory basis by both central and local government and private companies and landowners, particularly with respect to forest management and landscaping.

The Timber Growers United Kingdom 1960
A pressure group whose principal role is to promote and represent the interests of all private timber growers and woodland owners and to offer advice and marketing intelligence to its members.

Formed with assistance from the Country Landowners' Association and grant-aid from the Forestry Commission, it has some 2,000 members in England and Wales, who collectively own 70 per cent of all the private or dedicated woodland.

The group has a council, executive committee and four sub-committees covering training, technical, publicity and environmental matters.

It has good parliamentary contacts and is regularly consulted on forestry related legislation. It has helped to secure for timber growers various tax exemptions, without which forestry development would be unprofitable.

The group works in close liaison with the Country Landowners' Association and the National Farmers' Union.

Comment The forestry lobby is well organised and well connected. It is staunchly committed to commercial production and private ownership.

As a lobby, it has an extremely close working relationship with the Forestry Commission with which it enjoys many formal and informal links. What conflict does exist between conservationists and foresters seems to be absorbed principally by the Forestry Commission, leaving the voluntary bodies relatively free of controversy.

Addresses
Economic Forestry Group PLC,
Forestry House,
Great Haseley,
Oxford OX1 7PG

Timber Growers,
Agriculture House,
Knightsbridge,
London SW1X 7NJ

References
Hall, C. (1982) 'The Forestry Club', *ECOS, 3(1)*, 10–13
The Timber Grower, quarterly magazine of TGUK
Economic Forestry Group, *Annual Report and Accounts*

The National Farmers' Union
1908

Background Formed at a time of agricultural depression, originally as a network of county farmers' unions, the National Farmers' Union has become *the* national mouthpiece for the interests of farmers. The Union has 135,000 members representing over 80 per cent of all full-time farmers.

As a registered trade union, it has three basic aims: to protect and promote the interests of farmers; to advise and educate its members in all matters pertaining to farming; and to ensure the commercial viability of British farming.

It is made up of a federation of 49 County Branches (themselves derived from 860 Local Branches) with headquarters in London. It has a combined staff of around 840, and 29 specialist committees. Its budget for the year 1982–3 was £7,000,000.

Workings NFU headquarters has developed a close working relationship with the Ministry of Agriculture and has thus become an indispensable partner in the planning and implementation of agricultural policy.

The Union has extensive parliamentary links and is renowned for the acumen and proficiency of its lobbying.

The Union is closely involved with European agricultural interests and in EEC policy-making and has ensured that the majority of British farmers have benefited from Britain's membership of the Community.

County and local branches are concerned with advice and assistance to individual farmers; local secretaries administer the NFU's insurance scheme, liaise with the regional staff of MAFF's Agricultural Development and Advisory Service, and keep headquarters in touch with local farming opinion.

Comment The NFU is a formidable and highly co-ordinated lobby whose organisation, expertise and close relationship with government give it considerable power which groups, critical of agricultural policy, have been unable to match.

It has a virtual monopoly on representing farmers' interests to government so that it is very difficult for those within the industry who disagree with it, such as some of the smaller farmers, to gain a hearing. The Country Landowners' Association is the only other farming interest group with any significant degree of organisational effectiveness or influence. There is close co-operation between the two groups reflecting a considerable amount of membership overlap. The NFU is recognised as the senior partner and generally takes the lead on most matters of agricultural policy.

The Union has responded to conservationists' pressures by presenting farmers as the natural custodians of the countryside and stressing the need to retain the goodwill and voluntary co-operation of the farming community if practical remedies are to be found.

Address
Agriculture House,
Knightsbridge,
London SW1X 7NJ

References
Self, P. and Storing, H. (1962) *The State and the Farmer*, George Allen and Unwin, London
Grant, W. (1983) 'The National Farmers' Union: the Classic Case of Incorporation' in D. Marsh (ed.), *Pressure Politics*, Junction Books, London
Cox, G. and Lowe, P. (1984) 'Agricultural Politics and the Wildlife and Countryside Act' in T. Bradley and P. Lowe (eds), *Locality and Rurality: Economy and Society in Rural Regions*, Geo Books, Norwich
The British Farmer and Stockbreeder. The monthly magazine of the NFU (ceased publication, 1984)
NFU Insight, a bi-monthly briefing magazine
NFU, *Annual Reports*

The Smallfarmers' Association
1979

Background The Smallfarmers' Association was set up as a national body to promote the interests of medium and small-scale farmers and growers out of a concern that these interests were being neglected in agricultural policy-making. It is a group with only a few hundred members, 80 per cent of whom are family and small-scale farmers, although the membership is open to anyone supporting the Association's objectives.

The three formal aims are to promote the small family-type farm, to make farming more accessible to new entrants and to prevent the decline of rural communities.

The Association is opposed to the political and physical domination of agriculture by large-scale enterprises and the concomitant neglect of the interests of small-scale and family farmers.

It helped to set up the Tenant Farmers' Association in 1982, a body with about 1,000 members which exists to promote the interests of tenant farmers by lobbying for suitable tenure arrangements mainly concerning succession and tenants' rights, and by fighting rent reviews and the shrinkage of the tenanted sector.

Workings The Smallfarmers' Association performs no service function for its membership, but rather acts as a lobbying group — promoting discussion and making representation to Parliament and the Ministry of Agriculture, Fisheries and Food. It holds conferences and publishes documents on small farming policy.

The Association envisages the EEC's Less Favoured

Areas Directive as a framework for promoting the cause of small farmers. For such areas it seeks to establish a system of grants which would encourage small farms and place restrictions on the size of farms.

Comment In its short history, it has made some political impact, particularly during the passage of the Agricultural Holdings Bill (introduced into Parliament in 1983).

With the Tenant Farmers' Association it poses a potential challenge to the representational monopoly of the National Farmers' Union. However, they are as yet weak and marginal groups uncertain of what strategy to pursue to establish themselves as alternative sources of agricultural policy initiative. Their very existence, however, highlights and reinforces a polarisation of opinion in the farming community towards the structural and economic pressures confronting agriculture.

Address
The Smallfarmers' Association,
Room L1,
University of Reading,
1 Earley Gate,
Reading RG6 2AT

References
Tranter, R.B. (ed.) (1983) *Strategies for Family Work Farms in the United Kingdom*, Paper no. 15, Centre for Agricultural Strategy, University of Reading
Smallfarmers' Association, *Annual Report*

Farmers' Union of Wales (Undeb Amaethwyr Cymru) 1955

Background It was formed in West Wales as a breakaway group from the National Farmers' Union which was dissatisfied with the attention the NFU gave to the needs of Welsh hill farmers relative to the large farmers of the English lowlands. Its first President and General Secretary had been the Chairman and County Secretary respectively of the Carmarthenshire branch of the National Farmers' Union. It had a considerable struggle to establish itself in its early years against the hostility of the NFU and the indifference of the Ministry of Agriculture.

Indirectly, the rise of Welsh Nationalism in the 1960s assisted its cause. It has always been a strongly nationalistic organisation, distrustful of London-based institutions, though it has had no formal connection with political nationalism (or with any other political party).

The critical breakthrough for the Union came in 1978 after many years of campaigning against the agricultural establishment. In that year, as part of the general effort to devolve to Scotland and Wales the administration of certain functions of central government, the Secretary of State for Wales assumed full responsibility for Welsh agriculture from the Minister of Agriculture. This led to the establishment of the Agriculture Department in the Welsh Office and to the formal recognition of the Union

by the Secretary of State who agreed to consult with it on all matters of agricultural policy.

It represents a fairly distinct constituency: wholly Welsh and predominantly Welsh-speaking and almost wholly family farmers whose livelihoods are mainly in hill sheep and dairying. Its membership stood at 12,000 in 1984. It is organised into local and county branches (based on the former counties which existed prior to local government reorganisation).

Its income for 1983/4 was about £0.75 million. It employs about 60 staff.

Workings It has permanent committees representing milk producers, beef producers, sheep farmers and tenant farmers. Other committees cover land use and parliamentary matters, farm tourism, and agricultural and educational training.

It employs a network of county secretaries who administer the work of the county branches and give advice and information to members.

Since 1978, the Union has had a voice in the formulation of UK and EEC agricultural policies. This means that it is closely involved in price review negotiations but also in frequent consultations with Ministers and civil servants over all aspects of farming relevant to Wales.

It has concentrated its attention on furthering the interests of livestock producers. For example, it initiated the campaign to extend the Less Favoured Areas to allow farmers on the lower, marginal lands to qualify for similar subsidies as hill and upland farmers. It also played a prominent part in increasing the hill livestock compensatory allowances. The Union has always been a keen advocate of small family farmers. Its first policy document on their predicament was followed in 1959 by the introduction of a Small Farm Scheme to help small producers improve efficiency and attain economic viability. It has campaigned against various eligibility rules which bar many of the smaller farmers from access to grant-aid and other forms of support. In addition, it has championed the cause of the tenant farmer.

It is represented on various committees of the Welsh Water Authority, the Wales Tourist Board, the Agricultural Training Board and the Milk Marketing Board. It is involved with the Countryside Commission's Wales Countryside Forum and the county Farming, Forestry and Wildlife Advisory Groups.

It maintains strong links with Welsh MPs.

Comment The Farmers' Union of Wales is the only group to have successfully challenged the NFU's representational monopoly of the agricultural interest. In recent years it has established a *modus vivendi* with the NFU. The former, bitter animosity has been replaced by a keen sense of rivalry. On occasions, such as the defence of the Milk Marketing Board following EEC entry, the two Unions have collaborated in their lobbying efforts.

Over the years it has staunchly resisted many developments initiated by government bodies which it has seen as inimical to the interests of the family and hill farmers of Wales including: major afforestation schemes; the Rural Development Board proposed for mid-Wales in the late

1960s; the designation of a National Park in mid-Wales; and various other proposals for AONB and SSSI designations.

It considers that the Welsh family farm provides the best safeguard for the rural population and for the rural environment and that any threat to its future must be vigorously opposed. Under the category of 'threat' are included any externally-imposed conservation restraints. As one of its promotional pamphlets declares, 'we oppose the pressures for more conservation areas and more restrictions in existing conservation areas'.

Address
Undeb Amaethwyr Cymru,
(Farmers' Union of Wales),

Lys Amaeth, Queen's Square,
Aberystwyth, Dyfed SY23 2EA

References
(Y Tir) Welsh Farmer. The bi-monthly journal of the Farmers' Union of Wales. A special supplement to the April 1978 issue of the journal gives a history of the Union and the background to its achievement of government recognition.
Farmers' Union of Wales (1983) *The Uplands: A Charter for Wales* (Aberystwyth: FUW)
Farmers' Union of Wales, *Annual Report and Accounts* (Aberystwyth: FUW)
Wormell, Peter (1978) *Anatomy of Agriculture*, Harrap and Kluwer, London

Section 3.2
CONSERVATION

The British Trust for Conservation Volunteers
1970

Background The Trust's aim is to encourage and facilitate active public involvement in practical conservation work in rural and urban areas. It developed from the Conservation Corps which was established under the Council for Nature in 1959, to expand opportunities for volunteers in conservation.

It is a registered charity which employs 200 people. It is organised into 14 regions, 28 field bases and 314 local conservation groups which make up the volunteer force.

In addition to running practical conservation projects, such as tree planting, footpath clearance, wall repairs and canal maintenance, the Trust runs training schemes and residential working holidays.

Workings Its staff appoint field officers, provide training, negotiate funds and strive to increase the Trust's capacity to offer practical conservation work.

The Trust has established links with a number of Government Departments including the Department of the Environment and the Department of Education and Science. It is substantially grant-aided by Government.

It arranges day or residential work parties under trained leaders to carry out practical tasks for organisations including the Nature Conservancy Council, local authorities, the Royal Society for the Protection of Birds, the National Trust, the country trusts for nature conservation, and private landowners; a fee is charged to cover costs.

Its volunteers provide the labour force for projects and tasks. In 1982, this amounted to 125,000 workdays.

Comment A well-organised body, the Trust makes a valuable contribution to practical conservation as well as the promotion of environmental awareness. In one week in 1982, for example, its volunteers planted 50,000 trees. It has proved very popular with school and college students and many local groups are formed around individual educational establishments.

With assistance from the Manpower Services Commission, it has organised various conservation projects creating work for unemployed volunteers. This it sees as an increasingly important role, one for which it has undoubted government support.

Address
36 St Mary's Street,
Wallingford,
Oxfordshire OX10 0EU

References
The Conserver, The quarterly newsletter of the BTCV
Perring, F. (1983) 'The Voluntary Movement' in Warren, A. and Goldsmith, F., *Conservation in Perspective*, Wiley, Chichester
The BTCV issues a series of practical conservation handbooks on such subjects as hedge-laying and coppicing

The Civic Trust
1957

Background An organisation formed to encourage the protection and improvement of the built environment and to foster high standards of civic design and planning.

It acts as an advisory body to the 980 local amenity and civic societies (representing around 300,000 people) that are registered with it. It has no membership of its own.

It has a staff of 20. They are responsible to a board comprising mainly prominent industrialists and businessmen. It is financed by donations from business and industrial interests and grants from central government.

It promoted the Civic Amenities Act, 1967, which empowered local authorities to designate areas of special architectural or historical interest as Conservation Areas, and has encouraged local societies to monitor and protect such areas.

It runs the 'Pride of Place' awards which offer money to local societies engaged in conservation schemes, and the 'Civic Trust Annual Awards' which are for good design in new buildings and renovation.

Workings It administers various grants and funds on behalf of the Department of the Environment, including the Architectural Heritage Fund (which, in 1983, stood at £1.5 million) which assists building renovation and restoration, and a fund for small grants for improvement work in Conservation areas.

The Trust acts as part of the national environmental lobby over various planning and amenity issues. For example, with the CPRE, it has led the campaign to resist the raising of the maximum permitted weight for heavy lorries and the relaxation of planning controls. It has also been active in campaigns against derelict land.

The Trust has helped to initiate similar Trusts in the North East, North West, Scotland and Wales.

It has always tried to be a pacesetter and catalyst in promoting good urban design among the design professionals, amenity groups and local authorities. Over the years, it has helped to establish various experimental projects to demonstrate the creative possibilities of street improvement schemes, urban facelifts, land reclamation, pedestrianisation and the rehabilitation of run-down, historic areas.

It is increasingly involved in an educative and consultative role in administering the Heritage Education Group, set up by the Department of the Environment to bring together various interests in stimulating environmental education.

It is very active, through Europa Nostra, in promoting interest in and concern for Europe's architectural heritage.

Comment The Civic Trust is primarily concerned with urban conservation and design. The impact of the Trust in rural areas is largely through its many affiliated local groups who seek to protect the amenities of individual country towns and villages.

It is a conservation group that avoids many of the more contentious issues of contemporary conservation.

It enjoys considerable influence behind the scenes, particularly with the Department of the Environment.

Address
17 Carlton House Terrace,
London SW1Y 5AW

References
Barker, A. (1976) *The Local Amenity Movement*, Civic Trust, London
Heritage Outlook, monthly magazine of the Civic Trust
Lowe, P.D. (1977) 'Amenity and Equity' in *Environment and Planning*, A, Vol. 9, pp. 39–58
For an overview of the Civic Trust's first 25 years, see *Heritage Outlook* (July/August 1982)

The Council for National Parks
1977

Background The Council is a national voluntary organisation whose aims are to help protect the National Parks of England and Wales against inappropriate or damaging changes, to promote public support for and interest in them and to encourage their public enjoyment.

It was formed from and superseded the Standing Committee on National Parks which had been created in 1936, under the aegis of the Council for the Protection of Rural England to campaign for the establishment of the National Parks. Following the National Parks and Access to the Countryside Act 1949, the Standing Committee

settled into a watchdog role, opposing proposals for power stations, mining, reservoirs, new road and afforestation in the Parks, as well as pressing for greater independence and resources for National Park Authorities.

The Council was set up with financial support from the Countryside Commission when the CPRE was no longer able to staff and finance the Standing Committee. The Commission's grant enabled the new Council to employ its own secretariat and thereby operate independently from the CPRE.

The Council is composed of representatives from 30 constituent organisations, including the major national amenity, outdoor recreation and wildlife groups and the local watchdog groups for individual Parks. Three groups, the CPRE, the YHA and the Ramblers' Association, make the largest contributions to the Council's finance and play the biggest part in its work.

It has two full-time members of staff.

Workings The Council is regularly consulted by government on a wide range of issues potentially affecting the National Parks. It is also used as a source of advice on appointments to National Park Authorities. It has pursued an active role in lobbying over rural conservation legislation.

It enjoys a good working relationship with the Countryside Commission, often giving the Commission political support, or pursuing issues over which the Commission, as a statutory body, must be more circumspect or restrained. Recently it has established a 'Countryside Link Group' to co-ordinate consultation between voluntary conservation and recreation groups and the Commission.

It opposes development projects which its constituent groups consider harmful to the Parks. This is done by writing letters to National Park Authorities when they are considering planning applications or by giving evidence at public enquiries.

Comment It has managed to establish itself as an important group in the field of rural conservation. Its authority derives in part from its ability to speak for over 30 organisations with an interest in and detailed knowledge of the National Parks. It aspires to a central role in Park policy-making. If it were to achieve this, however, there might be internal strains between the divergent interests of countryside recreation, landscape protection and nature conservation which it comprises.

Its income is small and insecure and it badly needs additional financial support. In 1980 it launched 'Friends of National Parks' as a means of generating extra funds from individual supporters.

The Council sees its future as an authoritative forum for discussing National Park issues. As a result of the increasing politicisation of countryside issues, particularly since the passage of the Wildlife and Countryside Act, 1981, the Council has reluctantly recognised the need to adopt a more promotional and less reactive role. The publication in 1983 of two research reports critical of government policy towards National Parks is indicative of this new approach.

Address
4 Hobart Place,
London SW1W 0HY

References
Tarn and Tor, the Journal of the Friends of the National
Parks
For a discussion of the role of the Standing Committee on
National Parks see Sheail, J. (1975) 'The Concept of
National Parks in Britain', *Transactions of the Institute
of British Geographers*, Vol. 66, pp. 41–56
Herbst, L. (1983) 'To Promote or Protest' in *Ecos*, 4(2),
pp. 17–22

The Council for the Protection of Rural England (including the Council for the Protection of Rural Wales) 1926

Background The most prominent voluntary organisation concerned with protecting the rural landscape, it was formed (as the Council for the *Preservation* of Rural England) to co-ordinate a variety of rural interests and to promote legislation to preserve the countryside.

From the start it was well connected, with support among the political and cultural establishment as well as the planning profession. The idea for the new organisation was proposed by Patrick Abercrombie, the architect and pioneer town planner, who became its first honorary secretary. Other prime movers included its first President, the Earl of Crawford and Balcarres; and its first Vice-President, Guy (later Sir Guy) Dawber, an architect.

Within a year of its formation it had attracted as constituent members 24 established organisations, including (to name some which are still officially part of the CPRE) the Royal Institute of British Architects, the (now Royal) Town Planning Institute, the National Federation of Women's Institutes, and the Central (now Country) Landowners' Association. The CPRE was essentially a London organisation. Parallel county groups were soon established to pursue similar aims at the local level. By 1936 there were 26, most of them deeply enmeshed in the local county establishment.

It operates in three fairly distinct ways; one as a centralised lobby with a staff of 12; second, as a federal body with 33 constituent, national organisations; and third, as a national network of 43 autonomous county groups, with a combined membership of some 30,000 people.

The Council has developed a broad concern with the rural environment, embracing its traditional resistance to urban and industrial pressures and to any ill-sited or ill-designed developments, as well as more contemporary environmental concerns such as pollution control, nuclear power and agricultural intensification.

A separate Council for the Preservation (now Protection) of Rural Wales was set up in 1928. In most respects its organisation and activities parallel the CPRE, but on a smaller scale. It has 13 branches; 3,100 members; five staff; and 29 affiliated organisations (many of which are also constituents of the CPRE, but including others such as the Farmers' Union of Wales, the British Mountaineering Council and Undeb Cenedlaethol Athrawon Cymru — the National Association of the Teachers of Wales).

Workings Since its formation, the CPRE has consistently sought influence in the policy-making process. To this end it fosters informal links with civil servants, Members of Parliament and rural agencies such as the Countryside Commission. It and the CPRW are represented on the Department of Transport's Advisory Committee on Landscaping of Roads.

Much of the work of CPRE's headquarters' staff is taken up with monitoring national policies, commenting on official proposals with implications for the countryside, and encouraging protective legislation. In addition, they assist county groups in resisting major development schemes, particularly at public inquiries, such as the Sizewell B and M40 inquiries.

It has good and extensive links with journalists and a vigorous approach to publicising its concerns through the mass media.

It is active in international conservation, particularly through its membership of the European Environmental Bureau, the Brussels-based umbrella body representing environmental interests within the EEC.

In most rural counties the values promoted by the CPRE are strongly represented in local planning policies; and most CPRE branches are well-established within local government. A majority of them, for example, have a representative of the County Council on their executive committee, often the chief planning officer; and in return the CPRE is represented on official countryside committees where these exist. CPRE branches are also well represented on National Park committees. Most branches are automatically notified of planning applications for their consideration, and most are consulted, usually extensively, in the preparation of development plans. As well as strong formal connections with their county planning authorities, CPRE branches typically rely also on much informal contact and influence, with planning staff and sympathetic councillors. Their weak link is with District Councils. This has become a source of vulnerability to them as more and more planning powers have passed from the County to the District authorities.

Comment The Council's membership is drawn from the older, more well-to-do, rural residents, and in the past it has benefited from the social connections and prestige of its local and national committee members and officers. However, its distinctly upper middle class image has limited its popular appeal. In 1983, in the face of an ageing and stagnating membership, a new staff member was appointed, with financial support from the Countryside Commission, to recruit members in the urban areas in order to broaden CPRE's social and geographical base.

Through its history, its political objectives and tactics have undergone subtle changes. During the period up to and including the Second World War, it was a promotional group which contributed considerably to the creation of the post-war planning system. It led the campaign for areas of special protection in the countryside, including National Parks, and argued for the extension of town planning to the countryside, and for special controls on ribbon development and urban sprawl. Having achieved its major legislative aims, it settled down to monitor the new planning system to ensure it functioned effectively. During the 1970s it resumed a more active, campaigning role, taking stands on such matters as population growth, transport, agricultural development, energy and resource depletion, and showing renewed interest in instrumental and procedural issues, such as the conduct of public inquiries, improved public participation and defence of the planning system. It also altered its political tactics, adopting a more adversarial media-orientated approach to complement its former reliance on informal pressure and influence behind the scenes. The cause seems to be a combination of staff changes, competition from new, more radical groups and a decline in its traditional influence, due to public disillusion with the statutory planning system.

Parallel to these developments have been changes in the structure of CPRE, with a declining role for its constituent organisations. Indeed, on a number of issues it has taken up positions in direct opposition to its constituents. In the case of its opposition to the roads programme, this provoked the resignation of two of its constituents, the Automobile Association and the Royal Automobile Club, in the mid-1970s. Similarly, on the need for controls over agricultural development, the CPRE is at odds with the Country Landowners' Association and the National Farmers' Union. Constitutional changes during the 1970s have weakened the influence of the constituent organisations on the CPRE's council and executive committee and simultaneously have strengthened the representation of the county branches. Gradually, therefore, it has evolved from a federal, co-ordinating organisation to a unified, national pressure group.

Address
CPRE,
4 Hobart Place,
London SW1W 0HY

CPRW,
Ty Gwyn,
31 High Street,
Welshpool,
Powys SY21 7JP

References
Hall, C. (1976) 'The Amenity Movement' in C. Gill (ed.) *The Countrymen's Britain*, David and Charles, Newton Abbot
Lowe, P. and Goyder, J. (1983) *Environmental Groups in Politics*, George Allen and Unwin, London
'No Nukes in Ambridge? An interview with the director of the CPRE', *ECOS*, 1(4) (Autumn 1980), pp. 3–6
For the detailed operation of a county branch, see H. Buller and P. Lowe (1982) 'Politics and Class in Rural Preservation: a Study of the Suffolk Preservation Society' in M. Moseley (ed.), *Power, Planning and People in Rural East Anglia*, Centre for East Anglian Studies, Norwich

CPRE, *Annual Reports*
Countryside Campaigner, the magazine of the CPRE, issued three times a year
Rural Wales, the magazine of CPRW, issued three times a year

Farming and Wildlife Advisory Group (FWAG) 1969

Background The organisation aims to bring together farmers and conservationists to promote mutual understanding and co-operation. In Wales they are known as Farming and Forestry Wildlife Advisory Groups.

It was founded by a group of major countryside bodies including the National Farmers' Union, the Country Landowners' Association, the Royal Society for Nature Conservation, the Nature Conservancy Council and the Ministry of Agriculture, Fisheries and Food, following the Silsoe Conference in 1969, which was the first in a series of regional conferences convened to explore and demonstrate practical methods of reconciling farming and conservation

Central FWAG is a national forum of 23 members drawn from a variety of national organisations, with one full-time, paid Adviser.

There are 55 county-FWAGs. They strive for a membership balanced between farmers/landowners and conservationists. In some cases, the secretary and secretariat are provided by the county college of agriculture; in other cases these functions are performed by the Agricultural Development and Advisory Service of MAFF. They are also generally well supported by the county trusts for nature conservation. A number of county FWAGs employ their own full-time farming and wildlife advisers (grant-aided by the Countryside Commission) and others are likely to follow this initiative.

Workings The central body acts as a forum for informal contact and as an information centre. It publishes advisory notes for farmers on conservation techniques, sets up site visits to demonstration farms and organises conferences.

FWAG has assiduously avoided acting as a pressure group for conservationist interests; it takes no part in lobbying and avoids controversial issues, such as access. Its close working relationship with farmers, the agricultural lobby and government has been dependent upon this politically neutral approach. By its constituent groups, it is regarded as a high-level forum for the informal airing of matters of current concern.

FWAG has proved remarkably influential, not least because it enjoys the patronage of the MAFF. Other environmental groups, in contrast, have little influence with the Ministry.

County FWAGS, though independent, each mirror the national group in aims and activities — arranging farm visits and conferences and acting as a forum for discussion. Those groups which employ their own advisers are able to offer a consultancy service to farmers and landowners giving specific advice on how to conserve features of their land, and how to incorporate conservation objectives into their farm management plans.

Comment As agreement and conciliation become increasingly important in resolving land-use conflicts in the countryside, the already influential role of FWAG seems bound to grow.

Since the Wildlife and Countryside Act 1981, the farming lobby has had a strong interest in promoting the voluntary commitment of farmers to conservation as a means of staving off calls for the introduction of statutory controls on agricultural practices. The NFU and the CLA see the FWAGs playing a key role in this respect.

At the moment, most local FWAGs preach to the converted and have had little impact upon the vast majority of farmers and landowners who do not have a strong personal commitment to conservation. With sufficient encouragement and resources, though, the FWAGs could become a conservation version of ADAS. In 1984, a charitable trust was established to raise funds from voluntary, governmental and private sources to enable at least half the county groups to appoint their own full-time advisers within five years.

A prevalent criticism amongst conservationists is that in seeking to mediate between farming and conservation interests, the balance struck by FWAG is too heavily weighted in favour of the former. There is some strength to the criticism. The more radical conservation groups are excluded from FWAG so as not to upset the farming lobby, and even such groups as the CPRE and the Ramblers' Association have been excluded from the national body.

Address
FWAG,
The Lodge,
Sandy,
Bedfordshire SG19 2DL

References
FWAG (1982) *Farming with Wildlife*, Advisory Booklet

Friends of the Earth
1970

Background The most prominent of the new wave of international environmental groups, it advocates harmony between mankind and nature and unites the traditional interests of conservationists with more radical global concerns such as safe energy, species extinction, the wastage of natural resources and environmental pollution.

First established in America, there are now 24 independent, national FoE groups.

FoE UK comprises 250 local groups, 18,500 supporters and a national headquarters, which has a staff of 20 and advises and services the local groups as well as acting as the central policy-making body.

As a registered company and not a charity, it is free to lobby and campaign. Since 1979 it has been campaigning for the protection of British wildlife. It has sought to monitor and publicise damage to important wildlife habitats and has drafted and promoted a Natural Heritage Bill which would reform the agricultural support system and bring agriculture under planning controls.

Workings It has the best links with the newspaper and broadcasting media of any environmental group. Its campaigns are carefully planned to achieve the maximum media impact.

Its political style is an interesting blend of populism (stressing open campaigning and participatory action) and expertise (stressing its technical proficiency in disputing the wisdom of technological projects).

This leads it to pursue a variety of tactics depending upon the issue, including: organising recycling schemes; arranging marches, rallies and demonstrations; giving evidence at major public inquiries (such as Windscale and Sizewell); promoting private members' bills; lobbying Parliament; and consulting with Government Departments.

Comment FoE is undoubtedly the most successful of the new style environmental organisations that arose out of the student movement of the 1960s. It has broadened the range of environmental issues on the political agenda and the repertoire of political tactics available to environmental groups. Within this changed context, the traditional concerns of conservationists have acquired new significance and salience.

It has consistently striven to retain the individuality of its style and concerns and an independence of organisation to the extent that it rarely acts in a co-ordinated way with other environmental bodies except on a very informal level. This has contributed to its financial insecurity and a high membership turnover.

Consistently wary of political compromise, FoE has had to strike an often uncomfortable balance between participation in government and confrontation with government.

Address
377 City Road,
London EC1V 1NA

References
Lowe, P.D. and Goyder, J. (1983) *Environmental Groups in Politics* (especially Ch. 7), George Allen and Unwin, London
FoE issues a newspaper three times a year

The National Trust
1895

Background One of the oldest environmental groups, it was formed as a response to the increasing threat posed by industrial and urban growth to the countryside and ancient buildings of England and Wales. In 1907 it was reconstituted as a statutory body by Act of Parilament. It is now the most important non-governmental conservation body in the country with a membership of over 1.1 million people.

Although its aims of acquiring and protecting places of historic interest and natural beauty fulfil an important public role, it remains essentially a voluntary organisation, dependent upon a voluntary membership and donations, although it does receive much practical and financial support from government.

The Trust is unique among environmental groups in its relationship with the state. As legislation has been passed to preserve buildings and landscape, government has used the Trust's existing machinery rather than extend its own establishment. In return, the Trust has been granted various tax privileges and statutory powers, including the power to declare land inalienable.

It owns 1 per cent of the land of England and Wales, including 230 historic houses, a number of villages, 7.5 per cent of National Park land (including a quarter of the Lake District) and 655 km of coastline.

Workings Originally conceived as a promotional and lobbying group as much as a land trust, it has long since exchanged its pressure group role for that of a semi-public agency, reserving its considerable political strength for the occasions when its own property is under threat.

The Trust has a highly centralised organisation with a national Council of 52 members (part elected by the membership and part nominated by prominent cultural bodies and learned societies) and an Executive Committee of 28. Subservient to the Executive are 14 Regional Committees which handle the day-to-day affairs of the Trust's estate. The Trust's work is administered by a staff of 1,400. Its income in 1982 was £34.5 million.

It acquires land and property through legacies or from the Exchequer who have received them in lieu of tax debts or by direct purchase for which it depends upon membership subscriptions, appeals and grants from government and charitable trusts.

Comment The Trust is renowned for its management and presentation of historic houses, though it has been less receptive to modern techniques of recreation management and nature conservation.

The Trust has the closest links with government of any environmental group and government grants comprise about an eighth of its income. However, it has limited its overall dependency on public funds to avoid becoming vulnerable to bureaucratic or political pressures. In its promotional literature also, the Trust is always at pains to stress its independence. This is because its popular appeal hinges on its image as a voluntary organisation harnessing people's goodwill for a worthy cause.

The deliberate elitism of the Trust's decision-making structure makes it populist in appeal but not in its policy-making, from which its ordinary members are effectively excluded. Although very much dependent upon the membership for funds, it remains reluctant to see them as much more than visitors to its sites and passive supporters of its general aims. The decision — taken without reference to its membership or wider public discussion — to lease Trust land at Bradenham (Buckinghamshire) for the construction of a NATO command bunker caused considerable controversy and has led to pressures for the internal reform of the Trust.

Ultimately the Trust is an orgsanisation of immense importance in British conservation, though its ambiguous role as part voluntary organisation and part public agency does raise questions about the accountability of its leadership. Its conservatism and aloofness place it very much in the rearguard of the conservation movement.

Address
42 Queen Anne's Gate,
London SW1H 9AS

References
Lowe, P. and Goyder, J. (1983) *Environmental Groups in Politics*, Ch. 8, George Allen and Unwin, London
Fedden, R. (1974) *The National Trust*, Cape, London
National Trust Magazine
National Trust, *Annual Report and Accounts*

The Royal Society for Nature Conservation (formed 1912, as the Society for the Promotion of Nature Reserves)

Background One of the leading conservation groups, its objects are to promote the conservation of nature for the purposes of study and research and to educate the public in the understanding and appreciation of nature and the need for its conservation.

The Society was originally a small group of influential naturalists which sought to encourage the National Trust and rural landowners to establish nature reserves. The prime mover was Charles Rothschild of the famous banking family, who was a prominent Edwardian patron of natural history.

It was instrumental in persuading the government to create the Nature Conservancy in 1949 as an official agency to acquire and manage nature reserves, give advice on nature conservation and conduct ecological research.

The Society considerably altered its organisation, structure and aims in the 1960s and 1970s, to incorporate the burgeoning county trusts for nature conservation. It now exists as a federation of the 44 county trusts which collectively have 145,000 members and own or manage more than 1,300 nature reserves covering nearly 44,440 ha.

With the authority of national spokesman for the county trusts, it has broadened its role, diversifying away from the promotion of nature reserves and embracing a general concern for nature conservation.

It has a full-time staff of 26. In addition, almost all the county trusts employ their own staff.

Workings *The Society*. At a national level, the role of the Society is to represent the interests of the trusts in the legislative and policy-making field, and to promote public interest in nature conservation in general. Fundamental to this role is the 'client' relationship it enjoys with the Nature Conservancy Council which, in part, finances the Society and with which the Society shares many co-operative links.

It also has good parliamentary contacts. It services the All-Party Parliamentary Conservation Committee which is the main point of contact between MPs and Peers concerned with wildlife and the various environmental groups.

Its Conservation Liaison Committee brings together all the major statutory and voluntary conservation organisations to discuss their common concerns. Under the Committee's aegis a series of British Red Data Books have been prepared detailing the status of various rare and vulnerable species.

In conjunction with the *Sunday Times*, the Society runs WATCH, an organisation to interest children and teenagers in conservation and involve them in such projects as the Butterfly Countdown (Summer, 1981) and a census of dragonflies in relation to water pollution (Spring, 1982).

The County Trusts. The County Trusts acquire, manage and protect local nature reserves and Sites of Special Scientific Interest, and arouse local interest in nature conservation. They too work closely with the Nature Conservancy Council, particularly with its regional staff. Most enjoy strong links with local authorities and are frequently consulted on planning matters affecting wildlife and on the management of public land of conservation interest, such as local nature reserves, country parks and roadside verges. They give advice to Regional Water Authorities and to farmers and landowners about the management of wildlife habitats. They are also involved in providing nature study facilities for schools and colleges, and visitor centres and nature trails which interpret wildlife for the general public.

Comment More than 200,000 hectares of Britain are maintained by various organisations as nature reserves and for this achievement the Society can take much of the credit. When it was set up, the very concept of a nature reserve was novel. The Society provided the lead in convincing naturalists that the creation of reserves offered a practical means of protecting wildlife, and persuading government and public opinion that this was a desirable object, worthy of support.

Having helped in the setting up of the Nature Conservancy, the Society has had to adapt to its evolving role — often under pressure from the Conservancy — in order to maintain the close formal and informal links that exist between the two organisations. Now the Society acts in part as the Conservancy's voluntary arm, lobbying and working in areas where the other, as a statutory body, is constrained.

Like many federal organisations, the Society experiences tension between the centre and the county trusts, some of which are wary of the Society achieving too much power in relation to them. Its organisation faces other critical issues, including stagnation in the membership of a number of older county trusts and the radical challenge posed by the growing movement for urban wildlife conservation.

There is a certain amount of rivalry (as well as a great deal of co-operation) between the Society and the RSPB over the leadership of the conservation lobby. The Society sees itself as 'the only voluntary body concerned nationally with all aspects of nature conservation', and it has sought a central, co-ordinating role within the lobby. However, it is overshadowed in terms of power and resources by the RSPB.

Address
The Green,
Nettleham,
Lincoln LN2 2NR

References
Lowe, P. and Goyder, J. (1983) *Environmental Groups in Politics*, Ch. 9, George Allen and Unwin, London
Natural World, the magazine of the Society issued three times a year
Sheail, J. (1976) *Nature in Trust*, Blackie, Glasgow

The Royal Society for the Protection of Birds
1889

Background The largest wildlife conservation organisation in Europe and one of Britain's leading environmental groups.

The Society's basic aim is to encourage the conservation and protection of wild birds, particularly rare species, by developing public interest and legal protection and by promoting scientific research.

Originally formed to combat the fashionable millinery trade in exotic plumage which threatened the existence of various tropical bird species, it rapidly broadened its aims to cover general protection of birds. Its actions have successively encompassed: efforts to publicise and enforce bird protection legislation; campaigns to improve and tighten up the law; encouragement of public authorities and private landowners to establish bird sanctuaries; and direct acquisition and management of reserves by the Society.

Its membership, which stood at 8,000 in 1958, was more than 360,000 by 1983. Its Young Ornithologists' Club, established in 1965, has a further 110,000 members.

It has a permanent staff of 330. Its income for the year 1982–3 was £6,000,000.

Though it was 40 years before it acquired its first reserve, it now pursues a vigorous acquisition policy and owns or leases about 100 reserves covering about 50,000 ha.

Workings It has a long tradition of promoting wildlife legislation. Indeed, most bird protection legislation has been drafted by the Society. It also takes a general interest in any legislation affecting nature conservation. It has excellent parliamentary contacts.

It undertakes detailed ornithological research including the monitoring of population levels and, increasingly, the presence and distribution of pollutants, and the destruction of habitats. It organises Beached Bird Surveys whereby hundreds of volunteers scour beaches for dead seabirds as an estimate of the effect of oil pollution on their population.

Its expertise in bird conservation and its enormous popularity give it considerable authority with government departments, and it is usually closely consulted when the welfare of birds may be affected. It has close co-operative links with the Nature Conservancy Council.

It monitors threats to wildlife habitats and appears at public inquiries to oppose developments which threaten key sites.

It undertakes special protection schemes for threatened species such as ospreys, golden eagles and peregrines. It has a small team of investigators who work closely with the police, uncovering incidents of illegal trapping or killing of birds, or egg collecting.

It plays a leading role internationally in bird protection: for example, it was closely involved in formulating the EEC Directive 79/429 on the Conservation of Wild Birds.

It has an extensive educational programme which includes the Young Ornithologists' Club and a teacher's newsletter distributed to schools each term through local education authorities. The Society's Film Unit has an international reputation and its films are regularly broadcast on television.

Comment The conservation group with the biggest and broadest popular base, it has succeeded in marketing bird conservation as a good cause among armchair naturalists who are offered an attractive package deal. Their subscriptions support practical conservation work, and in return they receive the tangible benefits of a glossy magazine and privileged entry into the Society's properties.

In recent years, it has become more overtly political, willing to challenge other powerful groups, such as the field sports and farming lobbies and the water and forestry industries. Its expertise and popular backing are important resources, though its charitable status is a constraining factor.

Address
The Lodge,
Sandy,
Bedfordshire SG19 2DL

References
Birds, the quarterly magazine of the RSPB
Sheail, J. (1976) *Nature in Trust*, Blackie, Glasgow
Lowe, P. (1983) 'Values and Institutions in the History of Nature Conservation' in A. Warren and F.B. Goldsmith (eds), *Conservation in Perspective*, Wiley, Chichester

Wildlife Link
1979

Background Wildlife Link is a permanent liaison committee for various national organisations concerned with wildlife conservation. It provides a forum where its member groups can discuss national and international issues and co-ordinate political action on matters of mutual interest.

It was formed following the demise of the Council for Nature which previously had fulfilled a political co-ordination role for wildlife groups. The new Committee drew on the experience of a series of *ad hoc* coalitions of voluntary bodies which had come together to co-ordinate their lobbying over such matters as the Conservation of Wild Creatures and Wild Plants Act, 1975, the Endangered Species Act, 1976, and the annual meetings of the International Whaling Commission.

Initially it operated as a committee of the Council for Environmental Conservation (the umbrella body for the environmental movement), but became separate in 1983.

It comprises 33 voluntary groups, including the established wildlife groups (such as the RSPB and the Fauna and Flora Preservation Society) which composed the former Council for Nature; the new activist groups (such as Greenpeace and Friends of the Earth); and amenity bodies (such as the Youth Hostels Association and the Ramblers' Association).

The Committee has two members of staff.

Workings Its detailed work is carried out by five committees, each dealing with specific wildlife issues: endangered species, habitats, seals, whales and badgers.

It has developed a strong lobbying capability and has established its consultative status with the Department of the Environment, the Nature Conservancy Council, the Countryside Commission and the Ministry of Agriculture, Fisheries and Food.

Comment It proved effective during the passage of the Wildlife and Countryside Act, 1981, in uniting an often disparate nature conservation lobby. The impetus of that initial major achievement and the links and contacts forged at the time firmly established its central co-ordinating role and have served it well since.

It brings together a diverse range of groups which is both a strength and a weakness. A strength, because it incorporates such a range of expertise, political tactics and points of access to the political system. A weakness, because on some issues reaching a common line on which all the constituent groups could publicly agree may be a difficult and ultimately futile exercise. It works best, therefore, as a framework in which groups can keep each other informed and can informally co-ordinate their political activities and tactics. The demise of the Council for Nature (which was dissolved by its constituent groups) should be an object lesson against it acquiring a more dependent status or establishing its own authority apart from its constituent groups.

Address
Unit 22,
Finsbury Business Centre,
40 Bowling Green Lane,
London EC1 0NE

References
Cox, G. and Lowe, P. (1983) 'A Battle not the War: the Politics of the Wildlife and Countryside Act, 1981', *Countryside Planning Yearbook*, Geo Books, Norwich

RECREATION

Field Sports Organisations:
The British Association for Shooting and Conservation
The British Field Sports Society
The Game Conservancy

The British Association for Shooting and Conservation 1908

Formed originally as the Wildfowlers' Association of Great Britain and Ireland, it changed to its present name in 1981. It is the largest shooting organisation in the country.

Its threefold aims are to further the interests of the sport of shooting; to set and maintain standards of sportsmanship; and to conserve the countryside.

The Association has 60,000 members, 340 affiliated clubs, and 254 associated shooting syndicates for which it supplies information on habitats, game, guns and conservation, courses in gundog training and other related topics, legal advice, insurance and a land agency service.

As a national body, it has 20 full-time staff and 11 Committees dealing with a number of issues including research, management and conservation. A parliamentary committee maintains and services the Association's links with Parliament.

It has close links with other field sports organisations as well as with landowning interests. It has received grant-aid from the Nature Conservancy Council for its conservation work.

The British Field Sports Society 1930

The Society was established to represent and safeguard field sports interests and to resist the growing pressure to legislate against field sports.

It has 65,000 individual members and one-third of a million through affiliated Hunts and Clubs. At a national level, it has a strong parliamentary influence in association with the British Shooting Sports Council, lobbies for the interests of field sports and claims to have defeated 29 adverse Bills since its formation.

The Society is strongly defensive of field sports, and has established local action groups to counter opposition to hunting. A network of regional and local groups maintain interests at a local level.

The Game Conservancy 1970

The Game Conservancy was established as a management and research body pooling expertise in ecology, biology and estate management, with reference to game conservation. It was granted charitable status in 1980.

It has about 10,000 members, over half of whom are farmers and landowners. There are county regional groups.

The Conservancy is an authoritative body which has received funds from the Natural Environment Research Council for some of its investigations. Its work included a number of research, conservation and management projects aimed at reconciling the often divergent interests of farmers, foresters, naturalists and field sportsmen and women.

It offers a Game Advisory Service and arranges training and information courses primarily for gamekeepers.

Comment Like other recreational groups, the field sports organisations value the countryside as a resource and are keen that the resource should not be impaired. BASC and the Game Conservancy are actively committed to conservation — the former through establishing and managing wildfowl reserves; the latter through its research and practical advice on conserving habitats for game birds and animals. On its part, the BFSS, in its political defence of field sports, stresses their contribution to the enrichment and protection of the natural environment.

Long steeped in an upper-class image, the 'hunting, shooting and fishing' lobby is an influential group, with close ties with landowning interests.

There is marked ambivalence in conservation circles towards field sports. On the one hand, there is recognition of their positive contribution to the conservation of habitats and landscape — much of the remaining cover in the lowlands, for example, depends upon its value to landowners and sportsmen for hunting and shooting purposes. On the other hand, many conservationists are motivated by a concern for animal welfare and they have strong moral objections to any practical or political alliance with 'blood sports' enthusiasts. Finally, historical disputes over access to grouse moors has created an atmosphere of mutual distrust between rural amenity interests and supporters of field sports.

Addresses
British Association for Shooting and Conservation,
Marford Mill,
Rossett,
Wrexham,
Clwyd LL12 0HL

British Field Sports Society,
59 Kennington Road,
London SE1 7PZ

Game Conservancy,
Fordingbridge,
Hampshire SP6 1EF

References
ECOS (1983), *4(4)*, Special issue on conservation and field sports; see especially the article by Graham Cox 'A Sporting Chance for Conservation', pp. 2–9
Thomas, R.H. (1983) *The Politics of Hunting*, Gower, Aldershot
Shooting and Conservation, the quarterly journal of BASC
Country Sports, the journal of BFSS
The Field magazine
Shooting Times and Country Magazine

The Open Spaces Society
1865

Background The oldest environmental group, formed in 1865, as the Commons Preservation Society by upper-class, radical Liberals to preserve the commons of Victorian Britain for public enjoyment. The Liberal MP and land reformer, G. Shaw-Lefevre (later Lord Eversley) was the leading light, and John Stuart Mill was a founder member.

Previously known as the Commons, Open Spaces and Footpaths Preservation Society, it assumed its present title in 1983.

Through litigation and parliamentary action, it was able to stem the conversion of suburban commons into building plots and the enclosure of rural commons for agriculture. Early successes included the preservation of Hampstead Heath and Epping Forest. Its inability to acquire and own common land led it to promote the formation of the National Trust as a holding body. Since 1983 it has sought to acquire small areas of locally cherished common land that would not be of interest to the National Trust.

Its contemporary aims are to seek the preservation of commons, footpaths and open space, to promote new footpaths and secure public access to open land.

The Society has 2,800 members and an elected committee which includes MPs, Peers and committee members of other national environmental groups. Its annual income for 1982 was £40,000.

Workings The Society monitors threats to open land, footpaths and commons throughout Britain and is regu-larly consulted by the Department of the Environment and the Countryside Commission in this capacity. It advises local members over access rights and services the Central Rights of Way Committee, whose object is to co-ordinate action on the protection of public access. It is renowned as a source of expertise on the law relating to commons and rights of way.

The Society has been involved in securing and register-ing common land under the Commons Registration Act, 1965. It is now seeking a second stage of legislation to ensure public access to *all* registered commons and the provision of suitable management powers. In 1983 it stimulated the Countryside Commission to bring together various interests in a Common Land Forum to formulate recommendations for legislation. The Forum's secretariat is provided by the Society with financial assistance from the Commission.

Comment The concerns of the group are no longer cen-tral to the environmental movement and it has experi-enced dwindling support and influence over several years. Its function of promoting public access to the countryside has been eclipsed by the Ramblers' Association. Unlike the latter, it has no local structure through which to recruit support and combat threats to access.

Following its change of title, it has attempted to stage a comeback. The provisions under the Wildlife and Coun-tryside Act 1981, for public rights of way and definitive footpath maps have given it a new participatory impetus, while the acquisition of common land may become an important new function.

Address
25a Bell Street,
Henley-on-Thames,
Oxfordshire RG9 2BA

References
Williams, W.H. (1965) *The Commons, Open Spaces and Footpaths Preservation Society*, 1865-1965, The Open Space Society
Open Space, the Journal of the Society

The Ramblers' Association
1935

Background A major voluntary group concerned with promoting public access to the countryside.

The Association has three main aims: to encourage informal recreation in the countryside; to preserve the countryside; and to safeguard legal access.

It was formed as a federation of rambling clubs, many from working-class districts in northern England. Its early years were taken up with promoting the causes of a right of access to open countryside and the creation of National Parks and long-distance footpaths.

Today it has some 40,000 members organised into over 200 local rambling groups. It is a growing organisation — its membership doubled during the 1970s.

Workings *The National Council* and staff seek to safeguard the interests of ramblers in legislation and in the policies of bodies, such as the Countryside Commission, the Forestry Commission and regional water authorities. They retain a campaigning role and recently revived the issue of general right of access to privately-owned moorland. They also provide information and advice for ramblers.

The Association frequently unites with other national and local environmental groups in opposition to major development schemes in attractive areas of open countryside, and in promoting rural conservation policies with government and in Parliament. In these roles, it has developed very effective links with the media and a professional consultative style. It enjoys good parliamentary support particularly on the Labour side.

Local Groups are essentially rambling clubs, organising and participating in country walks and providing information about local footpaths. They also represent the interests of ramblers to local planning authorities, highway authorities and landowners, registering rights of way and monitoring any attempts to close or divert them. Increasingly they have taken on a management role, helping to waymark and maintain public footpaths.

Comment A growing and popular group, it is a recreational body with a strong commitment to scenic preservation — it promotes access but not mass tourism. This has brought it into conflict not only with farming and landowning interests, but also with other recreational bodies who see its influential, yet preservationist, role as being unrepresentative of rural recreational interests as a whole.

Address
1/5 Wandsworth Road,
London SW8 2LJ

References
Hall, C. (1976) 'The Amenity Movement' in Gill, C. (ed.), *The Countryman's Britain*, David and Charles, Newton Abbot
MacEwen, M. (ed.) (1976) *Future Landscapes*, Chatto and Windus, London
Ramblers' Association, *Countryside Briefing*
Rucksack, the magazine of the Ramblers' Association

Recreational Organisations in the Countryside:
British Mountaineering Club
Camping and Caravanning Club
Caravan Club
Cyclists' Touring Club
Youth Hostels Association

British Mountaineering Club 1944
The leading mountaineering group in Britain, its role is to promote mountaineering, to ensure standards and access and to protect mountain landscapes.

It is made up of 250 local groups, 240 affiliated organisations, 3,500 individuals and 40 trade organisations.

It is organised around eight Area Committees and a National Management Committee. In addition, it has a number of specialist bodies including the Amenity, Conservation and Access Committee which frequently joins forces with other voluntary organisations in opposing specific threats to mountain environments.

The Club is heavily financed by the Sports Council. It exists primarily to present a service to its members through training schemes, insurance, information, technical guidance and travel assistance.

It has purchased a number of rock climbing sites for use by member groups and is increasingly involved at a international level in the promotion of mountaineering.

The Camping and Caravanning Club 1901
The oldest open air group, the Club exists to encourage countryside recreation by protecting and promoting the interests of campers and caravanners.

It has a membership of 190,000 campers and caravanners organised into 13 Regional Councils. A National Council in London employs 36 full-time staff and is the central policy-making body.

The Club owns 45 camping sites and manages or leases a further 35 from private landowners and local authorities. Under the 1960 Caravan Sites and Control of Development Act, it has the power to license short-term, low density camping sites without the need for planning permission. It has a register of 1,000 such sites which offer secluded and simple facilities for club members.

The Caravan Club 1907
With 250,000 members (about one-third of all touring caravanners), it is one of the largest countryside recreational bodies.

Its role is to defend and promote the interests of the mobile caravanner. It provides its members with information, advice, insurance and, most importantly, access to Club-owned or leased camping sites.

The Club runs a total of 180 sites, 45 of which are owned, the rest being leased from a variety of private and public landowners.

Like the Camping Club, it is empowered to grant certificates to private landowners to establish small-scale caravan sites without the need for planning permission; and it has a register of 4,000 such sites.

The Club has sought to reconcile the needs of the caravanner with conservation and planning interests. The value of its expertise in the siting, design and management of caravan sites has been recognised by a number of local authorities and National Park authorities which have sought its help or advice.

There is a certain amount of rivalry between the Caravan Club and the Camping and Caravanning Club. Past efforts to amalgamate the two have not come to fruition.

The Cyclists' Touring Club 1878
The Club's object is to promote and protect the use of bicycles on public roads as a means of recreation.

With 35,000 members, the Club provides advice on cyclists' rights, deals with touring queries, provides insurance and technical advice and publishes scenic routes for cyclists.

District Associations maintain the club at a local level and organise group excursions.

In recent years it has become more politically active in pressing for improved provision for cyclists.

The Youth Hostels Association 1930
The principal hostelling body in the country, its function is to promote the enjoyment and protection of the countryside through the provision of cheap accommodation for walkers and cyclists, and through the encouragement of informal, countryside recreation.

The Association was formed in the inter-war years in response to a growing demand for inexpensive overnight facilities for ramblers and those on walking holidays. It now has over 250,000 members and owns or leases 284 hostels, many in the most attractive areas of the countryside.

Although its primary function is to provide accommodation for its members, 65 per cent of whom are under 25, it has long been concerned with environmental education. In recent years it has established 28 Field Study Hostels and has co-operated with the British Trust for Conservation Volunteers in sponsoring practical conservation work.

Similarly, since its earliest days, it has been an integral part of the rural access and amenity movements and maintains close links with all the major voluntary and governmental organisations concerned with rural conservation and recreation.

Comment The recreational bodies in the countryside exist basically to serve the interests of their members. They also identify with the general objectives of protecting the countryside and its amenities. Their involvement in those wider issues varies: the YHA is by far the most active, followed by the BMC; the other three tend to be passive supporters of specific groups or campaigns. All five groups, for example, belong to the Council for National Parks.

These organisations take various steps to ensure that the activities they promote blend in with the countryside including issuing codes of practice to their members, encouraging them to be sympathetic and considerate in their use of the countryside, paying careful attention to the location and design of new facilities, and making efforts to disperse recreational pressure from vulnerable over-used areas.

These organisations may also be of importance to conservation through the presence of their nominees on such bodies as the Sports Council, Regional Councils for Sport and Recreation and National Park authorities.

Although all these groups are committed to rural conservation, there exists the potential for conflict both among them and between their aims and the restrictive policies advocated by many conservation bodies. Their interests may occasionally seem to conflict with the interests of rural residents, landowners and farmers.

Addresses
British Mountaineering Club
Crawford House,
Precinct Centre,
Booth Street East,
Manchester M13 9RZ

Camping and Caravanning Club,
11 Lower Grosvenor Place,
London SW1W 0EY

Caravan Club,
East Grinstead House,
East Grinstead,
West Sussex RH19 1UA

Cyclists' Touring Club,
Cotterell House,
69 Meadrow,
Godalming,
Surrey GU7 3HS

Youth Hostels Association,
Trevelyan House,
8 St Stephen's Hill,
St Albans,
Herts AL1 2DY

References
Camping and Caravanning, the monthly magazine of the Camping and Caravanning Club
Clifford, J. and Lowe, P. (1980) 'The Caravan Club', *Vole* (March), pp. 35-8
Climber and Rambler, the monthly magazine of the BMC
En Route, bi-monthly magazine of the Caravan Club
Hall, C. (1976) 'The Amenity Movement' in Gill, C. (ed.) *The Countryman's Britain*, David and Charles, Newton Abbot
Hostelling News, quarterly magazine of the YHA
Oakley, W. (1977) *Winged Wheel: the History of the First Hundred Years of the Cyclists' Touring Club*, CTC, Godalming, Surrey
YHA (1984) *People, Places and Policy*, YHA, London

Section 3.4
SOCIAL

Rural Community Councils from 1920

Background These are county-based voluntary organisations whose objective is to improve the quality of life in rural areas.

The first RCC was formed in Oxfordshire in 1920. Now every non-metropolitan county in England and Wales has one, except for Norfolk. Their urban equivalents are called Councils for Voluntary Service.

They generally have limited individual membership, but rather one consisting of various social, welfare and environmental organisations within the relevant county.

The number of staff they employ varies from three or four up to more than a dozen.

On average, about half their income comes from the Development Commission (or, for the Welsh Community Councils, from the Welsh Office). The rest comes from local government and voluntary sources.

Workings Rural Community Councils vary greatly in size and in the functions they fulfil, but they have certain common features: for example, they frequently provide the secretariat for the county association of parish councils; they give advice on the provision and management of village halls and playing fields; they organise best kept village competitions; they act as agents for smaller voluntary organisations in negotiations with local authorities; and provide advice and information for their member organisations.

Since the mid-1970s they have been encouraged by grants from the Development Commission and advice from the National Council for Voluntary Organisations to assume a stronger role in promoting rural development and community initiative. Central to this change has been the appointment of 'roving' Countryside Officers. They have extended the work of RCCs into such areas as encouragement of villages to carry out appraisals of their social needs; promotion of public participation in planning; and assistance in the establishment of community transport and other self-help schemes.

All the English RCCs belong to the Standing Conference of Rural Community Councils (there is a separate standing conference for Wales). This provides a forum for exchanging views and information and a channel for consultation and lobbying on rural problems. It is serviced by the Rural Department of the National Council for Voluntary Organisations, which functions as an information and resource centre on rural policy and community self-help. The Development Commission relies on the advice of the National Council for Voluntary Organisations in allocating funds to the RCCs.

RCCs tend to have close links with organisations such as Women's Institutes, Citizen's Advice Bureaux, the Red Cross and volunteer bureaux. Many run the local branch of a national organisation, for example, of the National Playing Fields Association or the Council for the Protection of Rural England. They usually have close contacts with the County Council but more variable relationships with District Councils. The Standing Conference of Rural Community Councils is an active member of Rural Voice.

Comment The range and effectiveness of their activities varies considerably, depending largely on the size and quality of their permanent staff.

Traditionally RCCs have been worthy bodies, but rather marginal to the major social issues confronting rural areas and remote from the vast majority of rural residents. In the past few years a number of factors has increased their profile and pushed them into a more active and central role in rural development. These include the challenge of urban community development; the publicity given to rural social problems; the promptings of the Development Commission and the National Council for Voluntary Organisations, both of which see the RCCs as key catalysts in rural reinvigoration; and the influx of a more radical breed of younger and more professional staff with a social science or social work training (replacing staff who were typically retired armed forces officers).

However, they are, and are likely to remain, poorly equipped to act as very forceful pressure groups on behalf of the rural poor and deprived. They lack the staff and the appropriate structure to become a grass-roots organisation. Since their committees remain the preserve of 'the county great and the good' a paternalistic, consensual approach to rural problems is ensured. In addition, in contrast to the emphasis in urban community development on social welfare, social justice and political definitions of deprivation, RCCs are pervaded by an apolitical ethos of voluntary activity. Finally, the source of their funding is likely to place bounds on the extent to which they could adopt a radical or campaigning role.

Address

The address of the Standing Conference of Rural Community Councils is:

26 Bedford Square,
London WC1B 3HU

The headquarters of most RCCs is located in the county town.

References

Virtually all the RCCs issue a regular newsletter or magazine and an annual report.

Standing Conference of Rural Community Councils, *Annual Report*

Brasnett, M. (1969) *Voluntary Social Action*, National Council of Social Service, London

Rural Voice
1980

Background An alliance of nine national organisations brought together by the National Council for Voluntary Organisations to promote the interests of rural communities. Its members are the CPRE, the Country Landowners' Association, the National Farmers' Union, the Standing Conference of Rural Community Councils, the National Association of Local Councils, the National Council for Voluntary Organisations, the National Federation of Women's Institutes, the Agricultural and Allied Workers' National Trade Group of the TGWU and the National Federation of Young Farmers' Clubs.

Rural Voice's object is to ensure that government, the media and the general public understand the social and economic problems of those who live in the countryside (such as the poor provision of public services, housing and employment) and to encourage and assist its own member bodies in dealing with those problems.

Workings It acts as a forum for discussing social and economic matters in the countryside.

At a county level, it works primarily through the Rural Community Councils.

It has built up links with various rural bodies, including the Development Commission, the Council for Small Industries in Rural Areas, the Association of County Councils and the Association of District Councils.

It works mainly through its member organisations, encouraging them to raise and pursue issues of rural welfare with government departments and in Parliament.

It is serviced by staff of the National Council for Voluntary Organisations.

It has benefited from a dynamic, professional leadership and some early legislative successes, such as the safeguards for certain rural areas in the sale of council housing included in the 1980 Housing Act.

Comment In the past political and governmental interest in the countryside has focused on the exploitation or conservation of rural resources. Rural people have been neglected or ignored. The creation of Rural Voice was a welcome antidote.

However, it risks perpetuating a tradition of rural paternalism. Though it may claim to speak on behalf of rural residents, as yet it does not have a representative role. It lacks grass-roots support or involvement, though efforts are being made to establish local Rural Voices. More importantly, some of its constituent organisations are well entrenched in the rural power structure and benefit from existing policies; their interests are not necessarily the interests of the disadvantaged and deprived in the countryside.

There are potentially major disagreements between its constituent organisations and so far it has circumvented these by concentrating on problems of rural service provision and avoiding issues such as low pay in the countryside and land use conflicts. Unless it is prepared to tackle these more contentious topics, it is unlikely to become much more than a marginal talking shop.

Address

26 Bedford Square,
London WC1B 3HU

References

Rural Voice (1981) *A Rural Strategy*, NCVO, London

Rural Voice (annually from 1982) *State of the Countryside*, NCVO, London

Rural Viewpoint, bi-monthly magazine issued by the NCVO

Section 3.5
PROFESSIONAL

The Landscape Institute
1929

Formed as the Institute of Landscape Architects, it assumed its present title in 1978 in an effort to broaden its membership to embrace landscape managers and landscape scientists, as well as landscape designers. It acts principally as a standard setting body for these professions.

Its contribution to countryside matters derives essentially from the activities of its 2,000 members, rather than from its corporate influence.

It stresses both the scientific and the aesthetic elements of landscape design and seeks to promote the need for professional landscape advice in all rural and urban development.

The Institute is a constituent member of the CPRE and has recently lobbied for the statutory adoption of environmental impact assessment in major planning applications.

The Royal Institution of Chartered
Surveyors
1882

An old professional body whose members — as chartered surveyors and land agents — have long played an important role in rural land use decisions.

As an organisation, it is becoming increasingly involved in rural matters. It is a constituent member of the CPRE and has close links with the Civic Trust. It was a founder member of the Farming and Wildlife Advisory Group, reflecting the professional role of many of its 60,000 members in estate management. In addition, it is represented through its members on many countryside bodies.

It comprises seven divisions including a Land Agency and Agriculture Division and a Planning and Development Division.

The Royal Town Planning Institute
1914

The professional body for land-use planners, it acts as a watchdog over standards and practices, an advisory body for both the public and its members, a research and educational body and as a pressure group for planning interests.

The Institute has a membership of 12,800 planners, 70 per cent of whom are employed in central and local government.

It has a Rural Policy Committee through which it deals with countryside issues in response to government consultation or the initiative of its members, and through which it seeks to lobby both Whitehall and Parliament.

Comment The professional area of rural planning and conservation is not the exclusive preserve of any one profession or professional institution. Indeed, it is an area where a number of professional boundaries intersect and overlap, and so there is a fair degree of rivalry and competition between the respective professional institutions.

The three organisations here display considerable variation in their contribution to countryside policy. The RTPI is by far the most important of the three as an organisation involved in rural issues. It publishes policy statements and is consulted by those government agencies responsible for determining rural policy. The influence of the other two comes largely through those of their members who are highly placed or well respected.

The RTPI is committed professionally and ideologically to the statutory planning system and the role of its members in the countryside is almost exclusively derived from their employment in local government. The RICS, on the other hand, has responded to the increasing national emphasis on land management as an alternative to statutory control particularly among private landowning interests, where its involvement is more marked. Thus, whereas the RTPI is logically committed to statutory intervention, the RICS is more aligned to private initiative and a free-market philosophy. The LI is much smaller than the other two and less policy orientated, yet its publication, *Landscape Design*, illustrates the expertise of its members in landscape aesthetics, rural conservation and applied ecology.

All three institutions have a longstanding interest in the protection of rural amenity (for example, they are all constituent members of the CPRE). Occasionally, however, they have been in open conflict with conservation groups. For example, the RTPI and the CPRE were generally in opposite camps over plans for new towns.

Addresses
Landscape Institute,
12 Carlton House Terrace,
London SW1Y 5AH

Royal Institution of Chartered Surveyors,
12 Great George Street,
Parliament Square,
London SW1P 3AD

Royal Town Planning Institute,
26 Portland Place,
London W1N 4BE

References
Landscape Design, bi-monthly Journal of the Landscape
  Institute
RTPI News, monthly Newsletter of the RTPI
The Chartered Surveyor, weekly magazine of the RICS
The Planner, monthly journal of the RTPI

PART 4
Significant Documents

HAROLD BRIDGES LIBRARY
S. MARTIN'S COLLEGE
LANCASTER

Barlow Report
1940
Royal Commission on the Distribution of the Industrial Population

Background The Commission was appointed in 1937, prompted in part by a suggestion made by Sir Malcolm Stewart, the English Commissioner for the Special Areas, that the growth of industry in London was not due to 'hard economic factors', but was purely 'psychological' and therefore, could be altered as a result of Government action. He suggested that not only should there be more aid to the depressed areas, but an embargo on new factory building in London.

The Commission included representatives from law, the Civil Service, planning and architecture, economics and surveying. Some of these, notably Patrick Abercrombie and George Parker Morris, were to play a significant role in post-war reconstruction and development.

The Commission's terms of reference were to examine factors that had affected the present distribution of the industrial population together with possible future trends; to consider the social, economic and strategic disadvantages of having the industrial population concentrated into a number of large urban centres in particular parts of the country; and to suggest remedial measures that might be taken which were appropriate to the national interest.

Findings The Report found that national industrial and population growth had slowed down in the inter-war period, but with significant regional variations — the Midlands, and in particular London and the Home Counties, were growing in population and industrial growth was at a rate well above the national average.

Structural differences in the economic composition of the regions was responsible for their significantly different rates of growth and decline. The older areas were tied to fuel, raw materials and navigable waterways, whereas new industries were more oriented towards the market, and therefore had no reason to remain or establish in older coalfield areas. An increasingly large redundant population was left stranded. The Commission could see no reversal of this trend without Government intervention.

The Commission examined a number of issues in detail, including housing, public health, traffic congestion, journey to work, land and property values, but there was little theory or empirical research to assist them. The Report concluded that there was a need for specific remedies to overcome major disadvantages of conurbations, particularly London.

There was general agreement among Commission members about the conclusions drawn from the analysis of information collected, though there was disagreement in the remedies to be recommended. The most radical view was advanced by Abercrombie (an eminent architect and planner) that the Government should establish a ministry with new powers to control the location of new industrial development.

Other issues commented upon included: methods of preventing urban sprawl and loss of agricultural land through, in part, the development of a more effective town and country planning system; dealing more effectively with the linked issues of betterment and compensation. The Report suggested that there was a need for further investigation into such matters, an idea which was later undertaken by the Uthwatt Committee.

Comment The Barlow Report made a major contribution to the development of post-war planning in the United Kingdom. It was directly responsible, through a chain reaction, for the events that led to the creation of the whole complex post-war planning machine through the years 1945 to 1952. Its recommendations found favour with the radical administration of 1945. Its ideas of dispersing the industrial population undoubtedly influenced Lewis Silkin, the new Minister for Town and Country Planning, to set up the New Town Committee under Lord Reith in 1945, which led to specific New Town legislation in 1946. Although the first Conservative administration of the post-war period did little to encourage new town development, it did however, through the 1952 Town Development Act, provide financial aid and encouragement to local authorities for them to work out themselves how overspill should be dealt with.

References

Barlow, M. (1940) *Report of the Royal Commission on the Distribution of the Industrial Population*, HMSO, London

Hall, P. (1976) *Urban and Regional Planning*, Penguin, Harmondsworth

Ratcliffe, J. (1981) *An Introduction to Town and Country Planning*, Hutchinson, London

Cherry, G.E. (1974) *The Evolution of British Town Planning*, Leonard Hill, London

Uthwatt Report
1942
Expert Committee on Compensation and Betterment

Background The terms of reference of the Uthwatt Committee included making 'an objective analysis of the subject of the payment of compensation and recovery of betterment in respect of public control of the use of land'. The Committee was charged with a sense of urgency in that steps had to be taken so that reconstruction work during or after the end of the war should not be prejudiced.

The Committee was made up of three representatives from law (including the chairman) and two from the Institution of Chartered Surveyors with assistance coming from representatives of the Inland Revenue and the Estate Duty Office.

Findings The Committee did not recommend that all land should be nationalised, but rather that the development rights of undeveloped land should be vested in the state with all future land required for development being purchased by the state at its existing use value and then leased back at full market value; in so doing, the state would recoup betterment.

Where land was in the process of being developed, compulsory purchase should still take place but in this case there would be a need to pay compensation and this would be at the full development value.

Land actually developed would only be compulsorily purchased where it was necessary to achieve particular planning goals but even in these cases, compensation would be paid at a rate based on existing use in 1939; this was an attempt to overcome problems of excess speculation on land.

A levy was to be imposed upon all future increases in the value of land.

It was recommended that there should be money made available from central Government funds in the form of grants to local authorities to help them in the process of the redevelopment of central areas.

Comment The recommendations of the Uthwatt Committee played an important role in helping to fashion the 1947 Town and Country Planning Act in which were embodied the principles of central control over planning, development rights being vested in the state; and the requirement of planning permission prior to development, a levy being charged on the difference between existing and developed use value with existing use value the basis for compulsory purchase.

The whole question of betterment and compensation within the framework of statutory planning has caused bitter controversy between different political parties in the post-war period. Planning acts introduced by the Conservative Governments of the 1950s and 1960s reversed some of the regulations introduced in respect of compensation and betterment by the first post-war Labour administration. In the ensuing decades, successive Labour Governments introduced measures to tax development and thereafter Conservative Governments have relaxed such controls.

References
Ministry of Works and Planning (1942) *Final Report of the Expert Committee on Compensation and Betterment*, Uthwatt Report, HMSO, London
Ratcliffe, J. (1981) *An Introduction to Town and Country Planning*, Hutchinson, London

Scott Report
1942
Committee on Land Utilisation in Rural Areas

Background The Committee was appointed under Lord Justice Scott in 1941 by the Minister of Works and Building in consultation with the Minister of Agriculture. It included in its membership Professor Dudley Stamp, who had made major contributions to the understanding of the use and classification of land, and Professor Dennison, who was to write a minority report which was arguably a more accurate view of future land requirements of British agriculture.

The Committee's terms of reference were 'to consider the conditions which should govern building and other constructional development in country areas consistent with the maintenance of agriculture, and in particular the factors affecting the location of industry, having regard to economic operation, part-time and seasonal employment, the well-being of rural communities and the preservation of rural amenities'.

Findings The first part of the Report was devoted to providing a description and fact sheet of the nature of the land, the countryside and changes that had brought about land-use patterns and population distribution. Consideration was also given to the growing impact of urban growth and of townspeople on the countryside.

The first part of the report also looked at wartime and possible post-war trends in the use of rural areas. Some emphasis was placed on the dangers of returning to a pre-war situation when there had been insufficient control over development and land use in the countryside. The report advocated strong and unified control of constructional development.

The second part of the Report made the basic assumption that the Government wanted to see a vibrant and prosperous countryside, and that this end would be secured with the help of a central planning authority. Many positive recommendations were made in respect of housing, services, preservation of the countryside, industry and agriculture.

Agriculture was emphasised particularly in the Report and a call made for the development of a long-term plan which would include measures for the injection of capital, the maintenance of land in good heart and the establishment of stability in the agricultural industry. The Report advocated the retention of better agricultural land in farming, unless it could be proved that it was in the national interest for any change to take place.

The future role of planning by central and local agencies was detailed and certain procedures were recommended. These included national land planning; national zoning of land, including forest and recreational zones; the principle of 'onus of proof', where the onus was on developers to demonstrate that it was in the national interest for 'good land to be alienated from its present use'; the right of the state to acquire agricultural land compulsorily when it was in the national interest so to do.

Not all members of the Committee were in accord with all the recommendations in the report, and as a consequence, Professor Dennison issued a 'minority report' in which he took a broader economic view than the agricultural fundamentalists on the Committee. He indicated that improvements in agricultural productivity were capable of overcoming problems posed by the loss of land to development and thus agriculture need not be granted a prior right to rural land; planning rather than development should be the true function of Government; Government projects should be subject to planning control; the introduction of industry could be of considerable benefit to rural communities and that more effective planning was required rather than a new set of principles.

Comment The Scott Report had a major influence on land-use planning and policy formulation in the post-war period; it paved the way for the important 1947 Agriculture Act and influenced the 1947 Town and Country Planning Act and the 1949 National Parks and Access to the Countryside Act. Although the logic of the 'minority' view was less influential at the time it has found support in many quarters in the intervening period and has been advanced on numerous occasions in planning applications and planning appeals concerning the conversion of agricultural land to other uses.

References

Ministry of Works and Planning (1942) *Report of the Committee on Land Utilisation in Rural Areas*, HMSO, London

Gilg, A.W. (1978) 'Needed: a New Scott Report', *Town Planning Review*, vol. 5, pp. 352–71

Blacksell, M. and Gilg, A. (1981) *The Countryside: Planning and Change*, George Allen and Unwin, London

Dower Report
1945
National Parks in England and Wales

Background John Dower, an eminent planner, architect and conservationist, was requested to undertake a study of problems relating to the establishment of National Parks in England and Wales. His report was produced as a basis for discussion and was seen by Government as a preliminary exercise. Shortly after the report was published, the Hobhouse Committee was set up to consider Dower's findings and to make further recommendations.

Dower's work represented the culmination of two decades of debate on the question of National Parks. His report was issued at a time of rising optimism where there was growing interest in the concept of conservation in National Parks.

Findings Dower believed that a National Park should comprise an extensive area of beautiful and relatively wild country, where the aims should be: to preserve characteristic landscape beauty; to provide access and facilities for public open-air enjoyment; to protect buildings and wildlife; and to maintain established farming activities.

He drew up a list of suggested National Parks, which included many of the ones which were later so designated. A reserve list of areas which were suitable for designation as National Parks was also given, but only a small number were later included in National Parks. A third category included other amenity areas, not suggested as National Parks, some of which later became Areas of Outstanding Natural Beauty.

The report recognised two areas of potential conflict, the one between conservation and access, and the other between national and local need. In both instances, the pressure of a new wave of people coming to the countryside in greater numbers, in search of the physical and spiritual opportunities it had to offer, were seen as having a potentially damaging impact on specific land uses and on a rural way of life.

The Dower Report advocated a dual approach to change in National Parks. On the one hand, there was a need for strong development control to prevent development harmful to the broader objectives of the Parks and on the other, a need for strong positive action to undertake work to conserve, recreate and enrich scenic beauty and to develop facilities for both physical and passive recreation.

The maintenance of agriculture in National Parks was seen at the time as an important means of conserving landscape and the report recognised the need to foster understanding and co-operation between the farming community and the authorities if conflict between national and local objectives was to be avoided. Access was undoubtedly a problem — it was central to National Park objectives yet posed a threat to the farming community through damage and careless behaviour.

Wildlife and architectural conservation were given detailed consideration; the importance of both was stressed as having unique contributions to make to the intrinsic quality of National Parks. Various approaches to dealing with conservation were detailed, including the role of existing bodies, other volunteer help and the use of appropriate legislation.

Dower did not see any general reason for bringing the National Park land into public ownership and he appreciated the costs of doing so. Under some circumstances he saw public acquisition as being desirable if other forms of control or persuasion failed to achieve desired objectives.

Although Dower perceived the need for a national

authority and national guidance for National Parks, he did not believe that normal local government functions should be taken over as had been suggested in the Scott Report. Rather he advocated the joint committee approach; a National Parks Commission should evolve broad policy, provide advice and guidance and act as a link between the local committees and government departments.

Comment This was an important report concerning the future of recreation and leisure in the countryside. It formed the basis for the Hobhouse Report which in turn did much to guide the drafting of the 1949 National Parks and Access to the Countryside Act.

Many of the ideas in the Report provided the philosophical underpinning for subsequent legislation. The Report failed to anticipate the speed and nature of change in the post-war period, and it is arguable that with the benefit of hindsight, Dower might well have modified some of his views, such as those on agricultural development.

References

Dower, J. (1945) *National Parks in England and Wales*, Cmnd. 6628, HMSO, London

Cherry, G.E. (1975) *Environmental Planning 1939–1969. II: National Parks and Recreation in the Countryside*, HMSO, London

Ministry of Town and Country Planning (1947) *Report of the National Parks Committee*, Cmnd. 7121, HMSO, London

Hobhouse Report
1947
Report of the National Parks Committee (England and Wales)

Background The Committee was appointed in July 1945, by the Minister of Town and Country Planning to consider the Dower Report and decide which National Parks were to be selected, which were to be designated first, how to resolve boundary issues and what measures were needed to secure the objectives of National Park policies. The Committee was also invited to consider and make recommendations on other matters affecting parks, such as wildlife conservation.

The Report was required to set out a detailed scheme for the selection, planning and management of National Parks and also a supplementary plan for the protection of areas of outstanding natural beauty called Conservation Areas. The Committee was well aware of the difficulties involved due to the multiplicity of private and public interests and the complexities of town and country planning legislation which formed the legislative framework for its proposals.

Findings A central authority or National Parks Commission was to be established with a central headquarters and appropriate administrative, technical and clerical staff. Its first task would be the delimitation of the boundaries of twelve National Parks designated in the first three years following legislation. Each Park was to have its own Committee made up of representatives appointed by County Councils and the National Parks Commission.

All development proposals were to be subject to the permission of the Parks Committee, high design standards were to be required, derelict and unsightly land was to be cleared and mineral developments allowed only if national need was established. Other issues of national significance, such as forestry, power lines and military areas were to be referred to the National Parks Commission and kept under review.

A management approach was advocated which involved liaising with other agencies, government departments, farmers and landowners on matters such as traffic controls, the purchasing, leasing and negotiation of access to land, and the positive promotion of facilities for improved recreation, leisure and tourism.

It was accepted that not all areas in need of special protection — because of their landscape quality, scientific interest or recreation value — were in areas to be designated as National Parks. These other areas should be designated 'Conservation Areas' with appropriate powers and funding for their protection and the development of certain recreational facilities. Some were later granted AONB status, though not always afforded the degree of care and protection that had been envisaged.

The report appreciated that in some ways agriculture and forestry practice could interfere with the realisation of National Park objectives. It tentatively suggested that there should be some additional control over such operations but it contained an underlying belief that much could be achieved through reasonableness and negotiation.

Comment The Hobhouse Report formed the basis for the 1949 National Parks and Access to the Countryside Act.

The report made assumptions about the power of the National Parks Commission and the standing of that Commission in the eyes of other government departments which were not justified. It underestimated the rate of change in agriculture and visitor pressure on the Parks. Assumptions were made about reasonableness on the part of residents, farmers and land users which did not always prove to be correct. Thus the Commission and individual Park Committees had less power to control and manage development and land use in their pursuit of National Park objectives.

Not all National Parks and Conservation areas suggested in the Report were designated but, in those that were, despite the absence of sufficient formal powers and adequate finance, the National Parks Commission (later the Countryside Commission) and individual Parks have managed to achieve many of the goals identified in the Dower and Hobhouse Reports through careful negotiation and management.

References

Ministry of Town and Country Planning (1947) *Report of the National Parks Committee (England and Wales)*, Cmnd. 7121, HMSO, London

Dower, J. (1945) *National Parks in England and Wales*, Cmnd. 6628, HMSO, London

Cherry, G.E. (1975) *Environmental Planning 1939–1969. II: National Parks and Recreation in the Countryside*, HMSO, London

Gilg, A.W. (1979) *Countryside Planning: the First Three Decades 1945–1976*, Methuen, London

References

MHLG (1969) *People and Planning* HMSO, London

Sewell, W.R.D. and Coppock, J.T. (eds) (1977) *Public Participation in Planning*, Wiley, Chichester

Allison, L. (1975) *Environmental Planning: a Political and Philosophical Analysis*, George Allen and Unwin, London

Ratcliffe, J. (1981) *An Introduction to Town and Country Planning*, Hutchinson, London

Skeffington Report
Report on Participation in Planning 1969:
People and Planning

Background During the process of rapid change and redevelopment in the 1960s, there was increasing concern that planning was becoming alienated from the public — a theme noted by the Planning Advisory Group in 1965.

The Committee, under the chairmanship of Mr A.M. Skeffington MP, was appointed in March 1968, to consider the best ways of including publicity and securing public participation in the early stages of the preparation of development plans (structure and local) for any given area.

Findings There was concern that people should be kept informed during plan preparation, that there should be an adequate flow of pertinent information made available to the public and that local people should be made aware of the opportunities for participation.

Full participation was to be encouraged, but public debate should not be allowed to run on endlessly. People should be encouraged to do their own surveys so as to make better comment, provide better information about the planning process, its aims and objectives. The public should be kept informed as to what their elected representatives were saying, what they had achieved or why their ideas had not been accepted.

The Report recommended the appointment of community development officers and the encouragement of local forums for the purpose of discussion leading to the formation of neighbourhood groups.

Many of the findings were couched in broad terms and were often general in nature. The report acknowledged the fact that participation should go beyond planning, as planning was only a part of the Government system.

Comment The report promised much but, in retrospect, has delivered little. Whilst there was general support for the principles, there has been much subsequent criticism of the general nature of many of its findings and the naïvety that the participation process was not seen as political.

Government accepted the report in principle, but did little to implement its findings. Some of the ideas that were adopted were gradually dropped, such as the appointment of community development officers. The report did little to resolve the dilemma of, on the one hand, speeding up the planning process, but on the other, allowing greater but time consuming public participation.

Sandford Report
1974
Report of the National Park Policies Review Committee

Background The Committee, chaired by Lord Sandford, was appointed in 1971 by the Secretaries of State for the Environment and Wales, to review how far National Parks had fulfilled the purpose for which they were established, to consider the implications of the changes that had occurred (and could be expected to occur) in social and economic terms and to make recommendations as regards future policy.

The Committee membership was made up of people drawn from a wide range of backgrounds including the Countryside Commission, various Ministries, Trade Unions, County Councils and National Parks.

Findings The Report recognised the continuing conflict between the aims of preservation and enhancement of natural beauty and the aim of promoting access to and greater use and enjoyment of the recreational potential of the National Parks. It argued that there was a need to find more effective methods of reducing the conflict by developing better management, providing more education (and information), increasing and extending powers to afford better protection in critical areas and by using the powers of the 1968 Countryside Act, to develop facilities outside National Parks to act as counter attractions.

There was recognition that major mining and constructional projects posed a threat to National Parks. Attempts should be made to direct mining to other areas outside National Parks and to ensure that where construction projects were necessary, they were compatible with the purposes of the National Park and the character and location of particular sites as far as was possible.

A need was seen for park authorities to exercise a greater control over forestry operations including, where necessary and possible, the extension of formal planning controls. A broadleaved woodlands strategy was essential for amenity, wildlife and recreation.

The Committee felt there was a need to view agricultural change in terms of wider public interest and not purely from an agricultural point of view because of the threat of change to landscape, wildlife, access and amenity. It was seen to be desirable to achieve effective control by reaching agreement with the farming community but, where this failed, the Parks should be provided with compulsory purchase orders.

Conservation of natural beauty should take precedence where in conflict with other forms of development, including recreational projects. The impact of visitor pressure was noted, particularly the effects of private cars. Consideration was given to ways of reducing the impact of road improvements — the Committee suggested the removal of 'permitted development' rights.

The Report argued that National Parks objectives could be achieved by developing a better dialogue with all parties concerned. It suggested Parks set up advisory panels, and be granted powers to enter into management agreements with landowners, with powers of compulsory acquisition if all else failed.

Comment The report contains many innovative ideas which were generally welcomed by the Secretary of State and the Countryside Commission. Particularly important was the acceptance that conservation of natural beauty should take precedence over other developments and that there should be an extension of public ownership. However, the Secretary of State expressed some reservations about the report because of the financial constraints of the period. Government refused to agree to the extension of planning controls over forestry, road works and agriculture.

Although the Labour Government which fell in 1979 had lain a Countryside Bill before Parliament, new legislation was not enacted until 1981 — The Wildlife and Countryside Act — which gave National Parks additional powers to assist them in conservation and management work. However, there is some concern that without a significant increase in financial resources from central Government, National Parks may find it impossible to negotiate effective management agreements in pursuance of the conservation of wildlife, natural beauty and amenity. The objectives of National Parks in respect of conservation will be difficult to achieve unless there is a radical change in agricultural policies which encourage farmers to 'improve' land and boost output.

References

D.o.E. (1974) *Report of the National Park Policies Review Committee*, HMSO, London

D.o.E. (1976) *Report of the National Park Policies Review Committee. Circular 4/76*, HMSO, London

HM Government (1981) *Wildlife and Countryside Act*, HMSO, London

Blacksell, M. and Gilg, A. (1981) *The Countryside: Planning and Change*, George Allen and Unwin, London

Dobry Report
1975
Review of the Development Control System

Background George Dobry QC was appointed in 1973 to see if development control under the Town and Country Planning Acts met current needs, to see if the system could be improved upon, to review arrangements for appeal, and to set this in the context of local government reorganisation and consequent redistribution of planning functions.

Findings The main aim was to give greater freedom to 'harmless development' but to guard against 'harmful development' by retaining planning applications for all categories of development and then to separate out all applications which might have harmful effects. Thus there would be two streams — potentially harmful ones to which more detailed thought could be given and the rest which could be processed more rapidly. Main stream applications would be deemed granted if no decision was made within 42 days or transferred to the potentially harmful category within 28 days. Potentially hazardous applications would be considered within three months.

Speeding up of the development control process was to be helped by having more uniform procedures, more productive meetings with applicants, producing design guides and design briefs, and more delegation from councillors and committees to officers.

It was deemed necessary to make a better distinction between outline and detailed planning permission. A clearer distinction should be made between grounds of refusal in principle and objections of detail capable of resolution by negotiation. Following refusal the applicant was to be given the right of appeal.

The Report recommended only minor changes to the General Development Order, but suggested more use should be made of Section 52 agreements and Article 4 directions, and the use of impact studies ought to be introduced for certain categories of significant development. The idea that charges might be introduced for planning applications was also considered.

Comment The Report generally was welcomed though very little was acted upon immediately. Over time some of the recommendations have been adopted, for example, charges for planning applications were introduced in 1980. There is still an overriding belief by Government that development control is too restrictive and procedures too slow. Hence the gradual steps taken since 1979 to streamline the planning process. The concern that many people have expressed since the early 1970s, that the quality of decision was more important than the speed at which decisions were made, does not appear to be entirely shared by the D.o.E. who are increasingly concerned about the speed of decision-making.

References

Dobry, G. (1975) *Review of the Development Control System*, HMSO, London

Ratcliffe, J. (1981) *An Introduction to Town and Country Planning*, Hutchinson, London

Cullingworth, J.B. (1982) *Town and Country Planning in Britain*, George Allen and Unwin, London

Stevens Report
1976
Planning Control over Mineral Workings

Background The Committee was appointed in 1972 to

look at the way in which mineral exploitation was controlled under the provisions of existing legislation. All workings, reworking and aftercare and restoration were included in the scope of the report (though opencast coal was excluded as it was covered by specific legislation). The committee was also invited to make recommendations for additional or amended provisions and procedures.

The committee comprised only four members, but evidence was received from a large number of people and organisations.

Findings Because of the somewhat different nature of minerals operations, notably their impact and timescale, the committee felt that there was a strong case to be made for a special regime which separated them from run-of-the-mill development covered by existing planning legislation and procedures. Certainly the need to rethink minerals planning was long overdue: the 'Green Book', the main government guidance on minerals planning to local authorities, having been issued in 1960.

The role of the local planning authority (for minerals planning, the County Council) was vital if there was to be effective control and management of mineral exploitation. To this end, county planning departments should introduce minerals sections with specialist staff working full-time on minerals matters.

The Report saw a need to create a framework for minerals planning by developing long-term national policies for specific groups of minerals and to make sure these were reconciled with other national policies and land uses. Better liaison between government departments, relevant agencies and minerals planning authorities was necessary to help build up a more accurate picture of reserves and demand.

In dealing with specific applications, planning authorities should ensure that all affected parties are fully consulted. The report saw merit in reappraising the adequacy of the 21-day period during which objections to proposals could be submitted. It was felt to be equally important to ensure mineral reserves were not unnecessarily sterilised by other development.

A review of conditions attached to minerals planning applications was deemed important. This report suggested that minerals permissions should have a defined life of not more than 60 years; that the system of 'outline planning permission' should not apply for minerals; that county planning authorities should enter into agreements with operators in respect of working conditions and phased restoration; that there should be an indication of maximum output; and that ancillary activities which would require separate planning permission should be noted in the minerals application itself.

The Committee envisaged a need to have periodic reviews of conditions attached to a planning permission — it suggested every five years — and a review procedure was recommended to allow general public and interested third party views to be considered. They suggested that the powers to revoke or modify planning permissions under the 1971 Town and Country Planning Act should be retained.

Emphasis was placed on the need for effective restoration and where possible this should be progressive, be

monitored (in some cases supervised by the Ministry of Agriculture), and all done within the framework of the county's comprehensive policy for the restoration of mineral working.

The Committee felt that county policies relating to minerals exploitation and restoration should not necessarily remain static. Amendments should be possible and were probably desirable in the light of information received from central government departments about national policies, and as a result of improved technology and techniques for extraction and restoration.

Comment Government welcomed many of the recommendations of the Stevens Committee in its formal response and the report undoubtedly had a major influence in the formulation of the Town and Country Planning (Minerals) Act, 1981. It is likely that most of the detail contained in this report will guide the preparation and updating of a new 'Green Book' promised by central government on 'The Control of Mineral Workings'.

References

Committee Report (1976) *Planning Control over Mineral Working* (under the chairmanship of Sir Roger Stevens), HMSO, London

Blunden, J. (1975) *The Mineral Resources of Britain*, Hutchinson, London

Roberts, P.M. and Shaw, T. (1982) *Mineral Resources in Regional and Strategic Planning*, Gower, Aldershot

Verney Report 1976
Report of the Advisory Committee on Aggregates
Aggregates: The Way Ahead

Background The Advisory Committee on Aggregates was appointed in 1972 by the Secretaries of State for Environment, Scotland and Wales under the chairmanship of Sir Ralph Verney, to advise on matters pertinent to the supply of aggregates (bulk materials — natural or manufactured) for the construction industry. The Committee was also required to draw the attention of the Stevens Committee on Minerals Planning Control to sand and gravel issues, to consider whether further research was needed and whether further steps should be taken towards forming a policy for aggregates.

Findings Any aggregates policy should achieve an adequate and steady supply of materials to meet the needs of the construction industry at minimum economic and social costs with every effort made to reduce environmental costs.

The Report recognised that certain areas were under greater pressure than others, partly due to pressures for development and partly due to availability of resources. It raised questions relating to movement of mineral aggregate resources, the management of known aggregate resources and the effective assessment of demand.

The Report clearly saw a need for more effective ways of calculating demand to guarantee free flow of minerals and to avoid unnecessary exploitation. It recommended regular updating of statistics and stressed that forecasting should not rely too heavily on sophisticated analysis nor be projected too far into the future — 10 to 15 years was adequate. It saw a need for a more detailed assessment of resources particularly in areas of high demand.

Any imbalance between areas of demand and location of resources would result in increasing transport problems; therefore there was a need to consider improvements and adjustments to the existing transport situation and systems, and to consider less-used opportunities such as pipelines, conveyors and water transport. The transport question raised issues of efficiency of supply and impact on the environment.

The Report recommended that every effort should be made to improve performance in the restoration of land to productive use. The agricultural requirements raised important considerations of consultations with other agencies and bodies of expertise, such as the Ministry of Agriculture. The Committee felt that local planning had an important role to play in ensuring resources of aggregates were not sterilised by building development and in restoration programmes.

Alternative sources of aggregates should be considered — new land-based reserves, marine-dredged sources, use of wastes and recycled material.

A concern for the environment was a major feature of the Report. This was seen in terms of restoration recommendations and in consideration of the impact of new ventures such as marine dredging and, in particular, large-scale quarrying.

The Report stressed the need for a framework for policy and argued that this would at best be achieved through the work of regional working parties, constituted from local government and the minerals industry, who would undertake the essential work of resource identification and evaluation, consideration of the impacts of exploitation and demand assessment and forecasting.

Comment The work of the regional working parties has continued, though there is increasing concern that certain sections of the minerals industry no longer wish to play a significant role in this process. There are some indications in the early 1980s that planning decisions made on the basis of work done by the working parties is being overturned by the Secretary of State on appeal. Some concern exists among planning and environmental groups that much of the progress made towards more effective and rational minerals planning might be wiped out by the government's desire to remove obstacles to development as the state of the economy improves.

References

Advisory Committee on Aggregates (1976) *Aggregates: The Way Ahead*, HMSO, London
Committee Report (1976) *Planning Control Over Mineral Working*, (under the chairmanship of Sir Roger Stevens) HMSO, London
Standing Conference on London and South East Regional Planning (1974) *Sand and Gravel Extraction — the Regional Situation Policy Suggestions*, The Standing Conference, London

Roberts, P.W. and Shaw, T. (1982) *Mineral Resources in Regional and Strategic Planning*, Gower, Aldershot

Porchester Report 1977
A Study of Exmoor

Background Lord Porchester was appointed in 1977 by the Secretary of State for the Environment and the Minister of Agriculture, Fisheries and Food, following a request from Exmoor National Park Committee and consultation with the Countryside Commission, to make a study of Exmoor.

His terms of reference were to examine the amount of change in the moorland area of the National Park since designation in 1954, to consider the scale of future changes in the moorland and the implications of such change on food production, the economic and social interests of the area, and natural beauty and amenity in the National Park. He was also required to consider what courses of action were available to the appropriate public bodies 'to ensure that a proper balance is struck between the various and national interests involved; and the financial consequences of each.'

Findings The Report outlined the two contrary views relating to conservation of Exmoor; the one stressing the rare qualities of the moorland, which cannot be enjoyed elsewhere, and the other emphasising the need for land to be managed in the best interests of the farmer and the local community.

The report provided a context for its later deliberations by examining the historical evolution of Exmoor and by detailing its physical characteristics. The main activities on the moor were considered, conservation and recreation on the one hand, and farming on the other. This section also looked at Countryside Commission funding — motivated by conservation, amenity and public access and enjoyment — and agricultural funding — influenced by central government and EEC policies related to agricultural expansion.

Lord Porchester established that a significant proportion of the moorland was improvable for agricultural purposes, much of which was within 'Critical Amenity Areas', precisely where there was opposition to any change being permitted. Although ploughing had been a major cause of change, it was not the only reason for the decline of heather moorland — heather moorland was maintained through management and alterations to the management of the moor had allowed gorses and brackens to colonise and compete.

The Report accepted that there was a delicate balance between keeping enough moorland intact and giving the farmer enough land on which to farm satisfactorily. Converting moorland to agricultural use was expensive and most farmers would seek grant-in-aid from the Ministry of Agriculture. Because it was possible for grants to be withheld on amenity and conservation grounds, the role played by the Ministry's Agricultural Development and Advisory Service (ADAS) was critical. The Report concluded that there were areas of moorland where 'change from the traditional appearance should be resisted with the utmost determination'.

In considering what powers were available to protect the moorland areas from change in the Exmoor National Park, the Report acknowledged that some powers did exist under the 1949 National Parks and Access to the Countryside Act. But it reiterated the Sandford Report findings and felt that park authorities were virtually powerless to stop a farmer implementing proposals for change, and governments were not sympathetic to the idea of compulsory purchase of land. The Report looked at the possibility of a more extensive use of management agreements.

If an acceptable way forward was to be found, the Report concluded that there was an urgent need to secure heather moorland in critical and other defined areas for all time against conversion to agriculture. A number of steps were put forward: undertaking a major survey of the moor, introducing effective notification procedures prior to conversion, encouraging the Ministry of Agriculture to advise against conversion and withhold grant payments, giving National Park authorities powers to make Moorland Conservation Orders with suitable compensatory grants paid to the farmer for agricultural opportunities forgone.

Comment Some of the ideas put forward in this Report, notably 'Moorland Conservation Areas' were to have been included in legislation proposed by the Labour Government which fell in 1979. Subsequent countryside legislation introduced by the ensuing Conservative administration placed more emphasis on the attainment of conservation through the negotiation of management agreements.

Powers introduced in National Parks resulting from the Strutt Committee Report make it possible for the Park authority to block certain grant-in-aid to farmers from the Ministry of Agriculture, but these powers do not prevent the farmer undertaking improvement projects if he elects to do the work without government assistance.

Since the ploughing up of moorland on Exmoor became a problem in the 1960s, there have been pressures by the Park authority to have the Secretary of State impose an Article 4 Direction Order. Without a greater willingness on the part of Government to create the means of imposing restraint or by making money available for compensation, there seems little chance of halting agricultural incursions, unless economic factors dictate otherwise.

References

Lord Porchester (1977) *A Study of Exmoor*, HMSO, London

Blacksell, M. and Gilg, A. (1981) *The Countryside: Planning and Change*, George Allen and Unwin, London

Green, B. (1981) *Countryside Conservation*, George Allen and Unwin, London

Parry, M.L., Bruce, A. and Harkness, C.E. (1982) *Surveys of Moorland and Roughland Change*, Department of Geography, University of Birmingham, Birmingham.

Strutt Report
1978
Report of the Advisory Council for Agriculture and Horticulture: Agriculture and the Countryside

Background The Advisory Council for Agriculture and Horticulture in England and Wales, chaired by Sir Nigel Strutt, was asked in May 1977 to advise on ways in which the Ministry of Agriculture could help reconcile the national need for food production with other developing national interests in the countryside in the light of public interest in access, recreation, amenity and conservation. The committee had strong representation from the agricultural world, the chairman himself being a large landowner.

Findings It was felt that a sectional interest approach to the problem was only likely to heighten conflict between user groups, particularly as agricultural change would continue. Solutions could only be found if there were imaginative ideas, manpower, money and changes in attitude.

The Ministry of Agriculture could play a more innovative role, particularly through ADAS, and give better advice to farmers on matters pertaining to conservation, wildlife, and recreation and amenity. Better liaison with D.o.E., Countryside Commission, Nature Conservancy Council was required.

The Report argued that structure and local planning should be more explicit in respect of agriculture and say what priority was to be given to agriculture. D.o.E. officers should give more consideration to agriculture in plan-making and appraisal at the regional level. The Ministry should be consulted on planning proposals which affected areas in excess of five acres rather than the previous ten acres of agricultural land. The programme of sub-dividing Grade 3 agricultural land should be speeded up where critical land use planning decisions were likely to be made.

The Report saw scope for promoting better public understanding between town and country and reconciling agricultural and non-agricultural interests. To this end, MAFF and the Countryside Commission were identified as having a major role to play and it was felt that much could be achieved through a greater degree of inter-departmental co-operation at a central government level.

It was felt that much could be achieved to reduce pressures on key areas such as National Parks and the urban fringe by the improvement of warden services and the adoption of ideas generated through upland and lowland management experiments.

Comment The Report was produced primarily from an agricultural point of view but the committee attempted to adopt a non-partisan approach and saw many opportunities for changes of attitude and practice on the part of the Ministry of Agriculture and farmers.

Many of the views expressed in this report reflect ideas being considered by other groups and organisations concerned with rural matters, such as the Countryside Commission. Although not all the ideas were new, they were given a certain authority in that they were put forward by a group possessing an intimate understanding of the role of agriculture in the countryside.

The Report received a favourable response from the Minister of Agriculture, although there is little prospect of all the recommendations being implemented. Some have been acted upon, for example, the further subdivision of Grade 3 agricultural land, the extension of work on management in pressured rural areas and the need for planning agencies to consult with MAFF before permitting development on an area in excess of five acres.

References

Advisory Council for Agriculture and Horticulture in England and Wales (1978) *Agriculture and the Countryside*, The Council, London

Blacksell, M. and Gilg, A. (1981) *The Countryside: Planning and Change*, George Allen and Unwin, London

Green, B.H. (1981) *Countryside Conservation*, George Allen and Unwin, London

Northfield Report
1979
Report of the Committee of Inquiry into the Acquisition and Occupancy of Agricultural Land

Background The Committee was appointed in 1977 by the Minister for Agriculture, Fisheries and Food, in consultation with the Secretaries of State for Scotland and Wales. Its terms of reference were 'to examine recent trends in agricultural land acquisition and occupancy as they affect the structure of the agricultural industry'.

The Committee included representation from the agricultural industry and was assisted by specialist advisors in dealing with economic matters and the role of financial institutions in the farmland market.

Findings The Report noted that farm size was on the increase and that this trend was likely to continue. The increasing price of land was posing problems for young people trying to enter the farming industry. Taxation, economic pressures and issues relating to security of tenure were forcing landlords to take more land in hand or sell it to large financial institutions such as banks and insurance companies. The Committee found that financial institutions and overseas buyers owned only a relatively small proportion of Britain's agricultural land (1.2 and 1 per cent respectively) and as such no recommendation was made concerning governmental intervention.

No recommendation was made regarding any alteration in taxation to encourage the re-letting of agricultural land but some advantages were seen in modifying the effect of Capital Gains and Capital Transfer Taxes on landowners. Further amendments were suggested to allow VAT recovery on repair and maintenance on let land. No justification was found for any intervention in the control of land prices and rents.

The Report advised that more opportunities be created to facilitate the entry of young farmers into the industry. Local authorities should be encouraged to retain statutory small holdings or if they had to be sold then they should be retained as individual units. Private landlords were seen as having an important role to play in ensuring a healthy let sector though it was recognised that their numbers were falling. Some merit was seen in landowners turning over part of their land to some form of charitable trust and, in some cases, this should be in lieu of tax payments. Suggestions were made about modifying security of tenure legislation to guarantee the entry of better farmers into the industry and facilitate the retirement of older farmers. The Committee did not support the NFU view that tenants should have a pre-emptive right to purchase their farms, but agreed that they should be given three months' notice of sale by the landlord.

The majority of the Committee could see no justification for control over the size of holding. Increased public ownership of land was only to be encouraged where it replaced a 'missing rung' on the 'farming ladder', such as statutory smallholdings. The Committee saw some merit in introducing guidelines for agricultural landlords to cover a number of issues including social responsibility to the community and the locality. Under certain circumstances advantages were envisaged from the reintroduction of local development bodies such as the Rural Development Boards established under the 1967 Agriculture Act. A standing body to advise Ministers on developments in land tenure was suggested.

Comment Although successive governments have demonstrated a commitment to the retention of a healthy agricultural industry within the UK, there has been little indication that they have any intention of tampering with the industry as currently constituted. Some of the suggestions made by the Northfield Committee, for example the reintroduction of local development agencies, would be ideologically unacceptable to a Conservative Government.

Although the Report concluded that only a small percentage of agricultural land was owned by financial institutions, this position could change dramatically if it was perceived that there were major development opportunities to be realised or major tax advantages to be gained by large financial institutions and companies. This, in turn, might influence national productivity and the entry of young farmers into the industry.

References

MAFF (1978) *Report of the Committee of Inquiry into the Acquisition and Occupancy of Agricultural Land*, Cmnd. 7599, HMSO, London

Munton, R. (1979) 'The Financial Institutions: their Interests in Farmland' in *Report of the Committee of Inquiry into the Acquisition and Occupancy of Agricultural Land*, Cmnd. 7599, HMSO, London

MAFF (1977) *The Changing Structure of the Agriculture, 1968-1975*, HMSO, London

Sutherland, A. (1980) *The Northfield Report: A Comment* in Countryside Yearbook, Geo Books, Norwich

Report of the Planning Advisory Group 1965
The Future of Development Plans

Background The Planning Advisory Group (PAG) was set up by the Minister for Housing and Local Government and the Secretary of State for Scotland in May 1964 to review the planning system. This was felt to be needed in the light of growing criticism that the existing development plan system was out of touch with emerging planning problems and policies — the system was too slow and the end product was often too detailed in some cases, and insufficiently detailed in others.

Although the Group gave advice to departments on a wide range of planning related topics, its main concern was with development plans which were a key feature of the planning system. The Group saw a need to make them more flexible and more far reaching in time — perhaps 20 years and beyond.

Findings The Group argued that the planning system based on the 1947 Act was not adaptive enough to the rapid social and economic change of the 1960s. The system was losing credibility through slowness, lack of public understanding of planning aims and objectives and seeming lack of sympathy towards the impact of planning on individuals.

The Report advocated a two-tier planning system; one level to produce broad policy statements for a wider geographic area and a second level to produce more detailed local plans but in the context set by the former — hence structure and local plans.

Comment The *ad hoc* adoption by some local authorities of some of the main ideas contained in the PAG report resulted in the setting up of joint sub-regional planning exercises, such as the Nottingham and Derby, and the Coventry, Solihull and Warwickshire Studies.

In time, the Labour Government introduced a White Paper which incorporated some of the ideas of the PAG report and formed the basis for the 1968 Town and Country Planning Act (restated in the 1971 Act). There were five main proposals listed in the White Paper of which the most important to be embodied in subsequent legislation was the introduction of a new kind of development plan. Had the Redcliffe-Maud idea of 'unitary authorities' been incorporated in the 1972 Local Government Act, then it is arguable that the new style of development plans might have been more effective.

The Report had an influence in ensuring that the objectives of greater public participation were introduced into the 1968 Town and Country Planning Act and on the setting up of a Committee on Public Participation in Planning (Skeffington).

Criticism of the planning system has continued despite reforms which stemmed from PAG — these include inflexibility and alienation of public through slowness and insensitivity.

References

Planning Advisory Group (1965) *The Future of Development Plans*, HMSO, London

Ministry of Housing and Local Government (1967) *Town and Country Planning*, Cmnd. 3333, HMSO, London

Keeble, L. (1965) 'The Development Plan System, Planning Advisory Group's Report', *The Estates Gazette*, Vol. 195, pp. 472–3

Ratcliffe, J. (1981) *An Introduction to Town and Country Planning*, Hutchinson, London

Redcliffe-Maud, Lord (1969) *Local Government Reform in England 1966-9*, Report of the Royal Commission, Cmnd. 4040, HMSO, London

Ministry of Agriculture, Fisheries and Food
1966
Technical Report No. 11
Agricultural Land Classification

Background For nearly two decades the only national system of land classification was that produced in the early 1940s by Dudley Stamp. In 1962 the Research Group of the Agricultural Land Service — a division of the Ministry of Agriculture — held a conference to discuss the possibility of devising an improved system of agricultural land classification for the whole of England and Wales. The rationale was to provide more detailed information for the land use planning process.

A study group was set up comprising members from a number of divisions within the Ministry of Agriculture, the Meteorological Office and the Soil Survey of England and Wales.

The Director of the Agricultural Land Service gave the study group the following terms of reference: 'to consider and define requirements for an up-to-date agricultural land classification system, based on national standards, but capable of application to small areas' and 'to collect and process what relevant data there are and, where practicable, prepare agricultural land classification maps of a standardised kind'.

Findings Following preliminary considerations, the study group decided that the classification system would need to be objective, uncomplicated and capable of use by planners operating at both local regional and national scales. They decided to opt for a system which reflected long-term physical influences on crop production, namely site, soil and climate. As a second stage, it was seen as desirable to produce a supplementary classification based upon a range of economic criteria to give an indication of physical grades in financial terms.

For the physical classification of agricultural land, five grades or categories of land were recommended, ranging from Grade 1 where there were few if any limitations to agricultural use, through to Grade 5 where land was very poor and of little use for agriculture. Urban and non-agricultural land were separately identified and the information was issued in the form of maps at the scale of 1:50,000.

Other than some pilot exercises, little progress was made on the economic classification of land, despite the study group's belief that 'if applied with discrimination' an economic classification could provide valuable supportive information about the productivity of the physical grades. However, the study group maintained that economic factors should not influence the primary physical classification of agricultural land.

Comment The grading system based on physical characteristics was accepted by the Ministry of Agriculture and mapping proceeded quickly from 1966 to provide comprehensive coverage for the whole of England and Wales. The Agricultural Land Classification Maps have been used extensively by planners with a general presumption that wherever possible, development should not be permitted on the better grades of land, namely Grades 1 and 2.

Limitations of the maps have been identified, particularly in respect of farm practice and management and this is particularly felt to apply on Grade 3 land. Following the Strutt Report, it was decided to regrade category 3 into Grade 3a and Grade 3b in areas where the pressure for development was high with the hope that there would be a presumption against development on Grade 3a as well.

Although there is a belief that the maps have helped to protect some of the better grades of agricultural land from development, some commentators (for example, Boddington, 1978) have questioned the value of the land classification exercise and have made pertinent comments about its limitations, particularly its restriction to mapping physical limitations which have increasingly been outdated by technical developments.

In 1976, in England and Wales, there was 2.8 per cent Grade 1, 14.6 per cent Grade 2, 48.9 per cent Grade 3, 19.8 per cent Grade 4, and 13.9 per cent Grade 5 agricultural land.

References

Agricultural Land Service (1966) *Technical Report No. 11, Agricultural Land Classification*, Ministry of Agriculture, Fisheries and Food, London

Boddington, M.A.B. (1978) *The Classification of Agricultural Land in England and Wales: a Critique*, Rural Planning Services, Didcot

Agricultural Land Service (1974) *Agricultural Land Classification of England and Wales*, Ministry of Agriculture, Fisheries and Food, London

Forestry White Paper 1972 Forestry Policy

Background A review of forestry policy was undertaken in the early 1970s — its purpose was to re-examine forestry policy in the light of the fullest information obtainable about financial and social returns in present-day conditions.

The White Paper drew heavily upon an inter-departmental cost/benefit study produced in 1972 by economists from several government departments under the chairmanship of the Treasury — 'Forestry in Great Britain'.

Findings Despite environmental problems associated with timber production in upland Britain, performance was as good as anywhere else in temperate areas of the Northern Hemisphere, but timber production on its own was not economic.

Job loss through cessation of forestry operations in some parts of upland Britain would have a very serious impact upon the viability of communities. Thus an argument existed for continuing government aid to the Forestry Commission, and hence social factors became a justification for providing state aid to forestry.

The rate of return on investment was higher in hill farming than in forestry, but fewer jobs were created. The possibility of improving the return and increasing the number of jobs in forestry by further expansion of recreation was noted.

Recreational and conservation opportunities could be expanded through continued investment in forestry; this was not always quantifiable but was generally accepted as being in the national interest. The White Paper re-emphasised the Forestry Commission's obligations under the 1968 Countryside Act.

The White Paper acknowledged the financial difficulties faced by timber growers, given the length of time between planting and harvesting, but recognised the longer term potential of forestry in reducing heavy expenditure on timber and timber based imports. There was some speculation about the possibility of the introduction of a forestry policy within the EEC.

It was observed that private forestry also had a role to play in sustaining rural communities and providing further recreational opportunities. Government aid to private forestry should be continued but with some simplification of the various grant-aided schemes; measures should be taken to ensure that matters relating to amenity in private forests were adequately controlled.

Future government investment in forestry at current levels should be conditioned by the need to maintain population in rural areas and on the basis of the contribution made to amenity, conservation and recreation. Thus the Forestry Commission was seen to need a more flexible programme for the future.

Comment Some progress has been made in responding to many of the points developed in the White Paper, particularly in respect of conservation and amenity, but also through some simplification of the schemes for grant-aid to private forestry.

Some of the longer term hopes for the downstream processing of forest products have not materialised, giving rise to some debate about the need for aid to forest-based industries from the UK Government or the EEC Commission.

Under the provisions of the 1981 Forestry Act, parts of the Forestry Commission's holdings are to be sold. There is some concern that, given a degree of privatisation of state forestry, the benefits of policies operated since 1972 — where Government aid was motivated by job creation and improving recreational development — will be lost. Thus it has been argued that substantial privatisation of Forestry Commission holdings could have adverse social, economic and environmental consequences for many of the remoter parts of Britain.

References

HM Government (1972) *Forestry Policy*, HMSO, London

HM Treasury (1972) *Forestry in Great Britain: an Interdepartmental Cost Benefit Study*, HMSO, London

Miller, R. (1981) *State Forestry for the Axe*, Hobart Paper 91, Institute of Economic Affairs, London

Centre for Agricultural Strategy (1980) *Strategy for the U.K. Forest Industry*, CAS Report 6, The Centre, Reading

First and Second Reports from the Select Committee of the House of Lords on Sport and Leisure
1973
Sport and Leisure

Background A Committee was first appointed at the end of 1971, and then reappointed towards the end of 1972. Terms of reference were concerned with the demand for participation in outdoor sport and leisure out-of-doors and the removal of impediments to a fuller use of new and existing facilities.

The Committee included some members, such as Lord Redcliffe-Maud, who had experience of planning-related matters and two specialist advisers to the Committee, Professors Rodgers and Patmore, were also appointed.

Findings The Reports covered a wide range of pertinent issues, commencing with a deliberation on the nature of leisure time and the range of leisure and sporting activities available. They concluded that leisure time was likely to increase due to further reductions in the working week with the rider that demand on facilities would be concentrated and potentially uneconomic unless society could readily adjust accustomed work/leisure patterns. It was concluded that the relationship between supply and demand was not fully understood and that the techniques for effectively assessing demand had not been perfected.

The various bodies involved with the supply of sport and leisure were considered, ranging from various levels of government, to the private sector, to voluntary and *ad hoc* groups. Although the Committee viewed the public sector as the likely main provider of facilities in the future, it did foresee an important role for the private sector and a need for greater co-ordination between the various public agencies themselves as well as with the private sector in the future provision and funding of sport and leisure.

The Committee recognised the importance of finance and examined in some detail the funding and grant-aiding bodies, including local authorities, Sports Council, Countryside Commission and the budgets of other statutory undertakings with an interest in recreation such as the Forestry Commission. Important policy issues were raised such as the dilemma surrounding charging policies (free, partly subsidised or economically realistic), and recreational priority areas where it was believed that recreational opportunities were largely inadequate.

The Report gave varying treatment to a number of facilities. Water was considered as a separate issue at some length, as was leisure out-of-doors. Considerable attention was paid to leisure in the countryside, with only limited space being given to facilities relating to sport. However the important question of principles of provision was raised, namely that the greatest concentration of facilities should be closest to the greatest demand, with the proviso that there would be a supporting system of access by public transport.

Towards the end of their Report, the Committee gave consideration to a number of items which appeared to offer considerable potential for improving the provisions of sport and leisure in the future: the dual use of facilities, creating new opportunities through the reclamation of derelict land, better training facilities, staggering holidays, better publicity and building a greater awareness of leisure time into school curricula.

Comment This fund of information and ideas had a significant impact in that many of its ideas were incorporated in a Command Paper (Cmnd. 6200) presented to Parliament by the Secretary of State for the Environment in 1975, entitled 'Sport and Recreation' which in turn paved the way for a Department of the Environment Circular (47/76) 'Regional Councils for Sport and Recreation'. These new councils replaced Regional Sports Councils and attempted to create a more effective environment for a comprehensive approach to the planning, financing and management of sport and recreation, as well as the promotion of opportunities within different regions.

Although the work of the Committee paved the way for change in approaches to the provision of better opportunities for the enjoyment of sport and leisure, it did not find an effective solution to many problems, such as the conflict between recreation, amenity and agriculture in many parts of the countryside.

References

House of Lords Select Committee (1973) *First and Second Reports of the Select Committee of the House of Lords on Sport and Leisure*, HMSO, London

Department of the Environment (1975) *Sport and Recreation*, Cmnd. 6200, HMSO, London

Department of the Environment (1976) *Regional Councils for Sport and Recreation*, Circular No. 47/76, HMSO, London

Countryside Commission 1974 New Agricultural Landscapes

Background Concern about the impact that modern farming methods were having on the lowland landscape moved the Countryside Commission to sponsor a major investigation into the subject. The research was undertaken by two consultants, Westmacott and Worthington, and the project commenced in 1971 and lasted for 18 months.

The consultants were given a brief to examine 'how agricultural improvement can be carried out efficiently but in such a way as to create a new landscape no less interesting than those destroyed in the process'.

Findings The most significant change in the landscape was the loss of tree, shrub and hedge cover and this was taking place at a rate which was significantly greater than the replanting programmes which were being undertaken by local authorities and other agencies. The researchers believed that any attempts to further increase home-based food production would accelerate the rate of change in the appearance of lowland agricultural landscapes.

Considerable change had taken place in the lowland landscape in the post-war period, but the researchers felt that the impact of agriculture on the landscape in the ensuing decade to the mid-1980s would bring about a landscape change as fundamental as that brought about by the enclosure movement of the eighteenth century.

The landscape created by the enclosure movement was a functional one where trees and hedgerows served a practical purpose; Westmacott and Worthington observed that twentieth century farmers wanted to alter the landscape for equally functional reasons in that trees and hedgerows impeded modern farming practices. Because of this, landscape conservation would represent a

significant cost to the farmer and, therefore, could only be achieved through direct legislation, compensatory payments to farmers or through a major change of attitude on the part of the farming community.

The Report concluded that the value of the countryside could be measured in terms of wildlife, access for recreation and amenity, as well as in terms of agricultural production. However, farm accounts were only ever likely to show a limited return, if any, from conservation and recreation and this, therefore, was likely to be a major part of the impasse in the dialogue between the farming community and conservation groups.

Having accepted that agricultural activities would continue to modify the lowland landscape, the Report identified ways in which new and interesting landscapes could be created without undue interference with the requirements of modern farming practice. These included planting on naturally unproductive land, such as steep banks and verges or around farm buildings.

The Report indentified the need for a comprehensive approach to planning and managing the landscape if new landscapes were to be created which were capable of making a major contribution to wildlife, recreation and general amenity, without upsetting the nation's or individual farmer's agricultural objectives.

Comment Lowland agriculture landscapes have continued to change in the period since the Report was published, although the result does not appear to have been quite so dramatic as the Report intimated. The possible impact of change might have been lessened as a direct result of certain Countryside Commission projects, such as their Demonstration Farm Project, which was explicitly related to the New Agricultural Landscapes Report. Other action on grant-aid, tree planting and management and the negotiation of landscape agreements were undoubtedly influenced by this Report.

The 1981 Wildlife and Countryside Act can now be used to control very limited changes, but against this and the other Countryside Commission initiatives must be viewed the continuation of Government support for a prescribed level of self-sufficiency, together with the pricing and support mechanism embodied within the Common Agricultural Policy of the EEC, which encourage further intensification of production on the better-favoured land.

References

Westmacott, R. and Worthington, T. (1974) *New Agricultural Landscapes*, Countryside Commission, Cheltenham

Shoard, M. (1980) *The Theft of the Countryside*, Temple Smith, London

Davidson, J. and Lloyd, R. (1977) *Conservation and Agriculture*, Wiley, Chichester

Countryside Commission (1979) *Demonstration Farms Project*, Countryside Commission, Cheltenham

Agricultural White Papers
Food From Our Own Resources 1975
Farming and the Nation 1979

Background During the inter-war period there had been much Government concern about the decline in standards and output in British agriculture because it was becoming evident that the nation would have difficulty feeding itself from home produce in the event of war. To rectify the situation, legislation was introduced and some marketing boards set up to try to improve performance, guarantee prices, rationalise production and improve the physical quality of the land. During the wartime emergencies, the need to produce far more food resulted in a greater degree of control over production and a significant expansion of agriculture.

In the post-war period, government refused to allow British agriculture to fall into decline, giving many incentives and guarantees based upon the main provision of the 1947 Agriculture Act which demanded 'a stable and efficient industry, capable of providing such part of the nation's food as in the national interest it is desirable to produce'. This has remained the basis of agricultural policy for successive governments and had not been brought into question until entry into the EEC.

Findings 'Food from our own Resources' was produced at a time when there had been a sharp rise in the cost of imported foodstuffs and an equally sharp rise in the cost of fuel and fertilisers, which also raised the price of food. Government policy proposed, therefore, to create an environment in which farmers would have the confidence to increase and sustain production and which it was hoped, would give the nation some insurance against escalating food prices. It was argued that a policy of increased output from UK agriculture was justified on economic grounds, given the availability and cost of imported food and feed, irrespective of whether the nation elected to remain a member of the Common Market.

Although it was recognised that the case for expansion of output varied from one commodity to another, it was concluded that the industry had the capability to improve efficiency to achieve required targets. On economic grounds, improved efficiency and output would help reduce balance of payment deficits at a time when even higher food and feed costs were being projected. There was general agreement between government and the industry that if new targets of production were to be realised, then farmers had to be assured that the price support policies would continue to allow requisite forward planning and investment to take place.

'Farming and the Nation' was in no sense a contrary statement of intent to that propounded in the previous White Paper, but it was presented in the light of changed circumstances: the nation's decision to remain within the EEC, the government's greater control over the sterling price of agricultural commodities, massive inflation and adverse weather conditions in 1975 and 1976.

Both White Papers made reference to the wider industry, producers and processors, and the second White Paper also referred to the implications for rural employment and prosperity which depended so heavily upon the well-being of agriculture.

Both documents contained detailed information about the prospects for farming and associated industries, but of greatest importance is the fact that they represented a 'statement of intent and determination ... that the continued expansion of agricultural net product over the medium term is in the national interest'.

Comment These two documents were not well received by the European Commission who probably saw them as an attempt by the UK Government to influence the Common Agricultural Policy rather than adopt agricultural policies produced and ratified within the framework of the EEC.

Undoubtedly there has been a continued expansion in agricultural output since these White Papers were presented to the point where UK agriculture is now a major contributor to over-production within the EEC. Although farmers have been given considerable financial guarantees and aid through the policies of the UK Government and those embodied within the Common Agricultural Policy (CAP) it is far from clear that rural communities as a whole have benefited from agricultural policies introduced since 1975 particularly in respect of employment opportunities. It is also clear that there has been a substantial price to pay for agricultural expansion in terms of environmental damage and the loss of amenity.

References
HM Government (1975) *Food From Our Own Resources*, Cmnd. 6020, HMSO, London
HM Government (1979) *Farming and the Nation*, Cmnd. 7458, HMSO, London
Hill, B.E. and Ingersent, K.A. (1982) *An Economic Analysis of Agriculture*, Heinemann, London

Countryside Review Committee 1976 to 1979
The Countryside — Problems and Policies, 1976
Rural Communities: Topic Paper no. 1, 1977
Leisure and the Countryside: Topic Paper no. 2, 1977
Food Production in the Countryside: Topic Paper no. 3, 1978
Conservation and the Countryside Heritage: Topic Paper no. 4, 1979

Background Against a background of growing concern about the rate and nature of change in rural areas, articulated by influential individuals and pressure groups in the early 1970s, the Secretary of State gave approval to the setting up of the Countryside Review Committee in 1974.

The Committee's terms of reference were to review the state of the countryside and pressures upon it; to examine the nature and adequacy of existing policies relating to the countryside; and to consider changes in policies necessary to reconcile growing conflict in the countryside.

The Committee was an inter-departmental one, being chaired by the Department of the Environment and including officers from other related government departments. Although officers from some public agencies, such as the Sports Council and Countryside Commission, were allowed to serve on the Committee, there was no involvement of those who had orchestrated the demands for major government action such as the setting up of a Ministry for Rural Affairs or repeating the work of the Scott Committee.

Findings The first of these five papers attempted to identify the major activities in the countryside and the conflicts between different land uses and user groups and acknowledged a need to overcome conflict by achieving consensus and examining the possible ways by which management measures could assist. Central to its thinking was the concept of the multiple use of rural land and the view that all major agencies had to play a more effective role in resolving conflicts.

The first Report provided a platform on which the remaining our Topic Papers could build. For 'Rural Communities', the major arguments of employment and services were rehearsed, highlighting disparities between different parts of the countryside and within individual communities. For 'Leisure and the Countryside', the salient issues were listed including the changing nature of demand, the leisure opportunities afforded by the countryside — with more attention given to some issues which were deemed critical, such as public access and with many of the areas of the conflict identified. 'Food Production in the Countryside' examined trends in agricultural land loss, the conflicts between conservation and agriculture and identified two main problem areas, the uplands and the urban fringe. 'Conservation and the Countryside Heritage' looked at the main agencies involved in conservation work, identified the importance of 'Key Landscape Areas' and the aims of those involved with nature conservation, historic buildings and archaeology.

In each of the papers there are lists of summary recommendations which are not developed in any great detail, but with the need to overcome conflicts, gain consensus and encourage a fuller and integrated use of the countryside being repeated. Such recommendations that were made were produced as a basis for promoting discussion and comment.

Comment The Countryside Review Committee's work added little to the knowledge or understanding of rural problems, nor did its recommendations break new ground. At best, the Committee's work gave some measure of government support to the need to identify problems and conflicts in the countryside and to try to evolve policies which would overcome them.

The problems which were identified are largely still problems and there has been little lessening of conflict between many users of the countryside. Statutory measures have achieved little, particularly the Wildlife and Countryside Act, 1981, which arguably contains insufficient powers to acquire land or to make an adequate fund of money available for compensation. Despite an avowed commitment to lessening conflict in rural areas, successive governments have continued to pursue agricultural policies which have tended to aggravate rather than resolve areas of conflict.

References

Countryside Review Committee (1976) *The Countryside, Problems and Policies*, HMSO, London

Countryside Review Committee (1977) *Rural Communities*, Topic Paper no. 1, HMSO, London

Countryside Review Committee (1977) *Leisure and the Countryside*, Topic Paper no. 2, HMSO, London

Countryside Review Committee (1978) *Food Production in the Countryside*, Topic Paper no. 3, HMSO, London

Countryside Review Committee (1979) *Conservation and the Countryside Heritage*, Topic Paper no. 4, HMSO, London

Gilg, A.W. (1978) 'Needed: A New Scott Report', *Town and Country Planning*, Vol. 5, pp. 353–71

Countryside Commission 1976
The Lake District Upland Management Experiment

Background By the late 1960s, the Countryside Commission had become concerned that upland landscapes could become seriously impaired through the increasing pressures of tourism and recreation at a time when there were fewer people living in upland communities to undertake farm and country maintenance. The first stage of the Upland Management Experiment (UMEX) was carried out in Snowdonia and the Lake District between 1969 and 1972, and had the broad aims of landscape maintenance and improvement, trying to reduce farmer/visitor conflict and persuading farmers to adopt more positive attitudes towards conservation and recreation. The objectives for the second stage, carried out in the Lake District between 1973 and 1976, remained broadly similar though the project areas were enlarged and specific case study areas were identified.

A full-time project officer was appointed by the Lake District Planning Board which together with the Minister of Agriculture jointly sponsored the project. The project officer had an annual budget of £15,000 and could call upon the services of local farmers and contractors, voluntary groups and other suitable local labour to undertake necessary work.

Findings The role of the project officer was crucial as it proved to be the most effective way of liaising with the local community, particularly at trouble spots. Improving farmer/visitor relations was an important step forward in realising broader recreation and amenity objectives in the National Park.

Confidence in the experiment was boosted by the speed with which ideas and suggestions were translated into action on the ground; for example, improved car parking and the construction of new stiles and gates. The relative autonomy of the project officer in controlling his own budget speeded up considerably the time taken to undertake small-scale works — conventional local and central government accounting procedures would have resulted in greater cost and a time delay in implementing new works.

Originally it was thought that much of the work would be carried out by farmers or farm workers in spare time or slack times of the year. For some reason, this was not the case, even though many of the suggestions came from the farming community. Therefore, the project officer had to look elsewhere to find suitable labour and he found that there were still many rural skills to be found either on a full- or part-time basis. The benefit was, therefore, an opportunity to use project funds to generate some employment and also help to keep some country craft skills alive.

Fears that improvement works would attract more people, particularly to the more wild and sensitive parts of the National Parks, were not realised. Much of the work was concentrated on the lower hills where most of the pressures and conflicts had been identified.

The work of the experiment stopped short of moving into areas of work which had a very strong socio-economic character, though clearly this was seen as a logical extension of the work.

Comment Although the two stages of the Upland Management Experiment were justifiably deemed to be successful, they were really only successful to a limited extent. Many of the lessons learnt have been adopted in other National Parks and in experimental projects on the urban fringe, as in the Bollin Valley in Cheshire. The Hartsop Valley project attempted to carry UMEX forward and make positive recommendations about the ways in which more benefit might accrue to the upland communities. These included a co-ordinated approach by the grant-giving agencies and the local planning committee, the promotion of recreation and tourist accommodation and the payment of compensation to farmers and other local residents who suffer damage through any increase in recreation and tourism. Although the Upland Management Experiment made a worthwhile contribution on small-scale works, its organisation and budget were too limited to allow it to address itself to larger scale social and economic problems in upland communities. While the Lake District Special Planning Board have in fact upgraded the experiment to the Upland Management Scheme it remains uncertain how successful the ideas developed in UMEX will be on a continuing basis.

References
Countryside Commission (1976) *The Lake District Upland Management Experiment*, CCP 93, Countryside Commission, Cheltenham
Dennier, D.A. (1978) 'National Park Plans, a review article', *Town Planning Re*
Feist, M.J., Leat, P.M. and
Study of Hartsop Valle
Cheltenham

Nature Co

19

Nature Conservation an

Background During the late 1960s and 1970s, was growing in many quarters about the impact that agr cultural development was having on the appearance of the landscape and upon ecological systems. Under the 1973 Nature Conservancy Council Act the Council was charged 'to take account of actual or possible ecological changes' and to this end, through annual reports and discussion papers, it attempted to articulate concern about the damage that agricultural development was doing to natural systems.

Findings The first part of the Report was concerned with an appraisal of the implications for wildlife from the continued expansion of agriculture and of agricultural improvement. It identified the very close relationship between the intensification of agriculture and the loss of habitat and species: emphasis was placed on the need for nature conservation on the better grades of agricultural land where the pressure for intensification is greatest. The Report argued that the loss of habitat cannot be made good simply by establishing nature reserves on the poorer grades of land and stressed the need to conserve rich habitats because of the long time taken to regenerate diversity of species in newly created wildlife areas.

The second part of the Report looked at means by which the problems identified could be solved with a belief that wildlife should be seen as an integral part of the nation's heritage of natural resources and should be included in an overall strategy for land use in the countryside.

The Report accepted that agriculture would remain the dominant land use but in the same way that there was a presumption against development on the better grades of agricultural lands, so too important areas for nature conservation should be identified and similarly protected. The Report stated an obvious need for wildlife conservation areas in lowlands as well as in the uplands.

A number of approaches to dealing with conservation issues were suggested. These ranged from the wider use of methods employed elsewhere to the need for central and local government to set an example by adopting nature conservation objectives in the management of their own land. Also stressed was the need to provide better guidance, work out management agreements, and look at the possibility of financial inducements, compensation and tax concessions to farmers and landowners willing to become actively involved in conservation or forgo some of the financial advantages of agricultural intensification.

The Nature Conservancy Council believed that much progress could be achieved through a reappraisal of existing legislation and procedures and through a much greater involvement of the Council in consultations with

of Agriculture before grant-aid was given
...al intensification.

Since this initiative was taken by the Council,
...egislation has been introduced — the Wildlife and
...ryside Act 1981 — to help tackle some of the
...lems identified by this Report. A major criticism is
...at insufficient funds have been made available to allow
the Nature Conservancy Council and other bodies to
enter into effective management agreements with farmers.

Despite the efforts of the Council and other conservation pressure groups, it is far from evident that there is
widespread government commitment to the ideals of
nature conservation. Against a background of indifference and vested interest, it is difficult to imagine substantial progress being made in the field of wildlife
conservation in the immediate future.

References

Nature Conservancy Council (1977) *Nature Conservation and Agriculture*, Nature Conservancy Council,
London

Shoard, M. (1981) *The Theft of the Countryside*, Temple
Smith, London

Green, B.H. (1981) *Countryside Conservation*, George
Allen and Unwin, London

Countryside Commission
1980
Areas of Outstanding Natural Beauty: A
Policy Statement

Background The designation of land as an Area of Outstanding Natural Beauty (AONB) became possible following the enactment of the 1949 National Parks and Access
to the Countryside Act. Designation was the responsibility initially of the National Parks Commission and
subsequently, following the 1968 Countryside Act, the
Countryside Commission. There are currently (1984) 35
AONBs designated and confirmed by the Secretary of
State.

In 1978 the Countryside Commission decided to initiate
a major reappraisal of AONBs in England and Wales. To
this end they produced a discussion paper, arranged a
conference and commissioned a research exercise. The
Commission's Policy Statement drew heavily upon this
earlier work.

Findings The Countryside Commission concluded that
there was much support for the ideas of AONBs and that
consequently the process of designation should continue.
Problem areas were identified and much of the Policy
Statement is concerned with overcoming them.

The purpose of designation was seen as the conservation
of natural beauty, and (provided there was no conflict
with this prime objective) giving due regard to existing
land uses and to the social and economic needs of communities in such designated areas was deemed essential.

There was concern that in some AONBs there was
insufficient co-ordination between various local authori-

ties and interest groups resulting in inadequate management and planning. To overcome this problem the
Commission recommended that Joint Advisory Committees should be established to bring all interested parties
together and that an officer should be identified by the
local authorities to take an overview of the AONBs and
co-ordinate forward planning and management.

It was felt that in most AONBs there was a lack of any
clear statement as to what was the purpose of designation
and the subequent role of the AONBs. The Countryside
Commission was keen to develop means by which local
authorities could produce policy statements and also prepare effective management plans, if necessary with grant-
aid from the Countryside Commission.

In the context of statements of intent and management
plans, both of which it was recommended should be
related to statutory development plans, it was felt that a
more effective framework could be produced for exercising development control. The Countryside Commission believed that development control should emphasise
the conservation of natural beauty. Any development
permitted should be sympathetic to the objectives of conservation, and in the majority of cases large-scale
developments — including major road construction and
mineral extraction — should be excluded. Agricultural
notification procedures operating in National Parks should
be extended to AONBs and government departments and
agencies should improve consultation in respect of major
developments.

The Countryside Commission recognised the importance of finance and committed themselves to increased
expenditure on all pertinent aspects of AONB work ranging from the preparation of plans to the carrying out of
appropriate capital works such as landscaping and low-
key recreation provision.

Comment The process of designation has continued with
three additional AONBs being confirmed in late 1983 by
the Secretary of State. However considerable local opposition exists in many areas to the proposed designation of
more AONBs. This is the case in the proposed North
Pennines AONB where there is concern that designation
will result in an undue and unacceptable level of interference with legitimate local activities.

It seems unlikely that designation is likely to protect
natural beauty if the economic pressures for change are
present. There is no evidence to date that agricultural
notification procedures will be extended to AONBs or
that, if they are, they will necessarily prevent change.
There is every reason to believe that mineral operators
would be successful in obtaining planning permission, if
only on appeal — there are precedents from experience in
National Parks.

There are arguably inherent contradictions in the Policy
Statement's 'Purpose of Designation'. Experience would
suggest that 'safeguarding agriculture, forestry, other
rural industries and the economic and social needs of
local communities' are very often not compatible with the
primary aim of AONB designation, 'to conserve natural
beauty', nor the secondary objective of 'recreation'. It is
difficult to believe that without substantial political
support at local level, there is any guarantee of the objec-

tives of Areas of Outstanding Natural Beauty being realised.

In 1983 the Countryside Commission published a further policy statement on AONBs, generally following the lines of the original paper but taking into account new designations.

References

Countryside Commission (1980) *Areas of Outstanding Natural Beauty, a Policy Statement,* CCP 141, Countryside Commission, Cheltenham

Countryside Commission (1978) *Areas of Outstanding Natural Beauty, A Discussion Paper,* CCP 116, Countryside Commission, Cheltenham

Anderson, M.A. (1981) 'Planning Policies and Development Control in the Sussex Downs AONB', *Town Planning Review,* Vol. 52, pp. 5-35

Countryside Commission (1983) *Areas of Outstanding Natural Beauty: Policy Statement 1983,* CCP 157, Countryside Commission, Cheltenham

Countryside Commission, Greater London Council, Hertfordshire County Council
London Boroughs of Barnet and Havering
Urban Fringe Experiment
1981
Countryside Management in the Urban Fringe

Background The Countryside Commission has shown great interest in countryside management with investment in projects such as the Upland Management Experiment (1969) and the Lowland Management Experiment (1972). There has been a notable increase in funding for urban fringe programmes in the late 1970s and early 1980s.

There has been growing concern nation-wide about the urban fringe in respect of land use changes from agriculture to housing, industry and infrastructure, the loss of cherished landscapes, the appearance of degraded landscapes the loss of recreational opportunities and amenity, the conflicts between different recreational user groups, and conflicts in urban fringe objectives within and between local authorities.

Two experimental project areas were selected from within the Metropolitan Green Belt. The first was Hertfordshire/Barnet (October, 1976). Project officers and staff were appointed to run the two experimental projects; they were largely independent with their own budget, but were guided by steering committees.

The overall aim of the projects was to protect agricultural land, make a better use of waste land and to improve recreational opportunities. To this end, both projects set out to identify and analyse land management problems, to apply management solutions to the problems identified, to monitor the results and to provide appropriate feedback to interested bodies.

Findings To be effective, the countryside management approach requires a high degree of interaction with a wide range of interest groups (public and private) and individuals. The role of project officer and project team is critical, they need to be tactful, informed, sympathetic and innovative.

The presence of a project team can facilitate the carrying out of a range of small works quickly. This helps to create new opportunities and to reduce conflict. The team can give valuable feedback to the local authority to help them in turn to respond in a more sensitive and effective manner on key issues.

As the project team gains respect and wins confidence, it can play a key role in generating community interest on pertinent issues, receiving new ideas from the community and involving the community in work programmes, etc.

Comment The Countryside Commission believes countryside management offers real benefits to local planning authorities, farmers, visitors and local residents, amenity and recreation groups.

An increasing number of urban fringe management programmes are now underway, many with Countryside Commission support, such as Eston Mills in Cleveland and three projects in Tyne and Wear. Experience of projects and results of monitoring are being more widely disseminated. The Countryside Commission's Urban Fringe Experiment (UFEX) launched in 1980/1, is being expanded in the North West through the Groundwork Trust. The concept of the Groundwork Trust was introduced in 1981, in the belief that it was more appropriate for urban fringe projects to be handled by the private sector through means of a charitable trust than by local government departments.

Winning local confidence is still a key issue, particularly on private land, but more examples could be brought to public notice by improving performance on neglected public land in the urban fringe.

Political interest and willingness to support urban fringe schemes is vital if the countryside management approach is to be effective. Current government philosophy would wish to see more work done but for it to become self-financing through organisations such as the Groundwork Trust.

References

Countryside Commission (1981) *Countryside Management in the Urban Fringe,* CCP 136, Countryside Commission, Cheltenham

Countryside Commission (1983) 'The Groundwork Approach', *Countryside Commission News,* Issue no. 2, p. 6

Munton, R. (1983) *London's Green Belt: Containment in Practice,* George Allen and Unwin, London

Lavery, P. (1982) 'Countryside Management Schemes in England and Wales' *Planning Outlook,* 25(2), 52–9

INDEPENDENT REPORTS AND STUDIES

Land Use Surveys
1930, 1961
First Land Utilisation Survey of Britain
1930-49
Second Land Use Survey of England and Wales:
1961 onwards

Background Dudley Stamp's reason for organising the First Land Utilisation Survey was to find out exactly what use was being made of every acre in Britain; Alice Coleman's Second Land Use Survey was motivated to provide an updated version of Stamp's work and a basis for measuring the degree of land use changes that had taken place. Both surveys were carried out with the use of voluntary labour — school children, teachers and university students in the main — over a period of several years; the first aimed at achieving coverage for the whole of Britain, the second at England and Wales alone. The first survey was largely completed in the three years to 1933; the second survey was carried out throughout the 1960s and part of the 1970s.

Findings The First Land Utilisation Survey was mapped at a scale of six inches to the mile and presented at two scales, 1:63,000 (170 sheets) and 1:625,000 (2 sheets). There were six classes of use on this map: forest and woodland; arable land (with some sub-divisions); meadowland and permanent grass; heathland, moorland and rough pasture; orchards and nursery gardens; chief urban areas.

The Second Land Use Survey was mapped at a scale of six inches to the mile and published at a scale of 1:25,000 and by 1973, 107 sheets were available out of a possible total of 843 for the whole of England and Wales. These maps had 13 categories of land use: settlement, industry, transport, woodland, water and marsh, derelict land, open space, grassland, arable, market gardening, orchards, heath and rough land, unvegetated areas. There were further sub-categories and sub-classifications, making a total of 70 different types of land. The six-inch manuscript maps for the whole of England and Wales are available for consultation at Kings College, University of London.

On both survey maps, the major land uses were distinctively coloured and interpretation was helped by, in the case of the First Land Utilisation Survey, an explanatory memoir for each county, a major undertaking in itself and a unique record of land use in the 1930s and 1940s and for the Second Land Use Survey, a Land Use Survey Handbook was published.

Comment The surveys attempted, with varying degrees of success, to provide accurate land use information, but unlike the classification produced by the Agricultural Land Service, which was concerned with representing long-term land capability, the land use survey maps only provide information about land use at a point in time. As such, this makes them of little value, other than as historical documents, and of virtually no importance either to the Ministry of Agriculture or the planning agencies. They also suffer from having been carried out by an inexperienced team over a long period of time during which processes of urbanisation and agricultural change made them an inaccurate record, in some cases by the date of their publication.

The First Land Use Survey undoubtedly helped Dudley Stamp to produce his Land Classification of Great Britain in 1944; the maps and commentaries were used by the Scott Committee, of which Stamp himself was a member. The Land Use Survey remains an important and classic historical document and provides a basis for measuring land use change since the 1930s.

In a similar way, Coleman's Second Land Use Survey provides a detailed land use record and the six-inch manuscript maps are still frequently consulted by botanists, ecologists and geographers. Alice Coleman's continuing studies into land use are now linked to the Land Decade Educational Council (LAND) whose objectives are to 'work for conservation and to encourage improvements in land use in both town and country'. LAND is a group of influential people, notably landowners and architects, registered as a charity and committed to a fundamentalist view of land use issues.

Such extensive land use surveys are unlikely ever to be repeated; students from various disciplines concerned with land use are not trained in the interpretation of air photographs, which to the trained observer can yield a wealth of information.

References
Stamp, L.D. (1962) *The Land of Britain: Its Use and Misuse* (3rd edn), Longmans Green, London

Coleman, A. and Maggs, K.R.A. (1965) *The Land Use Survey Handbook* (4th edn), Second Land Use Survey, Isle of Thanet Geographical Association

Boddington, M.A.B. (1974) 'Sources of Agricultural Data' in Edwards, A. and Rogers, A., *Agricultural Resources*, Faber, London

Coleman, A. (1976) 'Is Planning Really Necessary?' *Geographical Journal*, vol. 142, pp. 411-37

Coleman, A. (1982) 'A Chain Reaction of Land Misuse in Britain', *International Journal of Environmental Studies*, vol. 19(2), 91-5

The Countryside in 1970
1970
Proceedings of the Third Conference

Background The Countryside in 1970 Conference was initiated by the Duke of Edinburgh in 1963, and for a period of seven years, including three conferences, a diverse body of people and organisations embarked upon an exercise of considering the most effective way of protecting the countryside from unwarranted change and degradation but, at the same time, allowing its potential to be realised for a much broader cross-section of the population.

Findings The Report clearly drew very heavily on the experience and writings of the previous seven years: the earlier work is summarised at the commencement of this document. What were seen as the major themes were identified: agriculture and forestry, urbanisation and the countryside, social issues, leisure, responsibilities for the environment and finally choices and opportunities. Three special issues were raised in the report: people, economic considerations and the international dimension of conservation.

One of the important conclusions from this period of work was that investigation and debate should not cease but continue with the aim of reporting to another conference within several years. It was felt that, with strong leadership, there was a force to be harnessed which could influence change and policy-making in rural areas for the good. In looking to the future, the then Director of the Nature Conservancy stressed the need to resolve the problems of conflict in the countryside with the simple, but stark view: 'destroy our environment and we cannot survive'.

Comment It is difficult to evaluate precisely the contribution made by the Countryside in 1970 to conservation and conflict resolution in the countryside. It certainly fired the imagination of many and it cannot go without note that during the seven-year period, a major policy statement was made ('Leisure in the Countryside') which in part paved the way for the 1967 Countryside Act for Scotland and the 1968 Countryside Act for England and Wales. This legislation created a framework in which the more limited objectives of the 1949 National Parks and Access to the Countryside Act could be broadened and extended to the countryside as whole, with a new agency — the Countryside Commission — to co-ordinate and fund a wide range of conservation and recreation work.

References
Secretariat of the Standing Committee (1970) *The Countryside in 1970; Proceedings of the Third Conference*, Royal Society of Arts, London

Zuckerman Report
1972
Report of the Commission on Mining and the Environment

Background The Commission was set up on the initiative of a consortium of mining companies in 1971. This was not a governmental commission, but its establishment was undoubtedly stimulated by the Conservative Governments' (1970-4) desire to stimulate a fuller use of the mineral resources of the UK. Growing public concern about the impact of mining on the environment was also given as a reason for setting up this Commission and it was hoped that ways might be established by which conflicts between mining and conservation might be reconciled.

Countryside and conservation interests were strongly represented on the Commission which was given the brief of considering all aspects of exploration, mining, reclamation and after use and making recommendations designed to reconcile mining activities with other areas of national policy, particularly those concerned with physical planning, amenity and conservation.

Findings The Commission concluded that minerals should be dealt with in the same way that planning dealt with other development, but with certain modifications for non-ferrous metals. The General Development Order should be amended to include the first stage of exploratory drilling — even in National Parks, AONBs and other areas enjoying special protection — but subject to conditions of the 1963 GDO. A code of practice should be approved by the Secretary of State. It established need for a right of appeal by local planning authorities and in some cases, the right to impose additional conditions. Later stages of drilling should require planning permission.

Public inquiries — more likely in designated and protected areas — should deal with the merits of drilling and not in the first instance with the later stages of mining. If mining companies could provide all the necessary information about drilling and mining at the same time, then one public inquiry should deal with both phases. In advance of a public inquiry there should be a statement of pertinent facts agreed, where possible, by all parties.

Where information was inadequate, base line studies should be produced and maps of areas enjoying special protection ought to be regularly updated to indicate the nature of planning policies and the degree of protection afforded. Broader public discussion was needed on the subject of mining and the environment with wide representation from all interested parties, and mineral companies were recommended to provide more information for the public during the evaluation stage of mineral development.

Great attention should be paid to all aspects of rehabilitation; landscape programmes needed to be ready prior to any on-site works and regularly updated and, in addition, a plan produced to guarantee satisfactory re-establishment of vegetation cover. It was recommended that mining companies consider ways of guaranteeing that funds were available to carry out all phases of restoration — a renewal trust fund was suggested, not dissimilar to the Ironstone Restoration Fund established under the provisions of the 1951 Mineral Workings Act, where mining companies paid an agreed sum of money into a fund for every ton of mineral extracted — this to guarantee that money was available for restoration.

All reasonable steps should be taken to avoid pollution problems both during mining operations and afterwards. The Commission stressed the need to look at all aspects of pollution when planning and undertaking mineral works and to provide adequate and appropriate training for mining engineers to enable them to cope with the varied consequences of mining.

Comment This was a very thorough Report which attempted to make workable recommendations some of which (for example, improved planning procedures and more effective restoration) were reconsidered in the context of the Stevens and Verney Committee Reports.

Although the Commission had been set up as an initiative of private mining companies, there is nothing in the Report to indicate that it was in any way biased in favour of the mining industry and the membership of the Commission would have helped to guard against any such accusation.

Since the Commission published its Report, major new legislation has been enacted in the form, for example, of the Town and Country Planning (Minerals) Act, 1981. Progress towards effective control over major mining developments has been slow but the Zuckerman Report certainly made a valuable contribution.

References

Zuckerman, Lord (1972) *Mining and the Environment*, Commission on Mining and the Environment, London
Blunden, J. (1975) *The Mineral Resources of Britain*, Hutchinson, London
Roberts, P.W. and Shaw, T. (1982) *Mineral Resources in Regional and Strategic Planning*, Gower, Aldershot
Commission of the European Communities (1980) *Proposal for a Council Directive Concerning the Assessment of the Environmental Effects of Certain Public and Private Projects*, COM(80)313 Final, The Commission, Brussels

Essex County Council 1973
A Design Guide for Residential Areas

Background The Essex Design Guide was produced in the light of growing dissatisfaction with the character of much of the post-war suburban development. It was described as having 'a dreary suburban uniformity' and lacking 'specific Essex characteristics'. These general criticisms were levelled at both developments in and around villages.

The aim of the new policy was to 'establish a planning framework within which a more varied and imaginative approach to area housing design can be fostered' with the end product being 'housing schemes which are better to live in and to live with'.

Findings The Written Statement which accompanied the First Review of the County's Development Plan set out the new development control policies for residential areas. There were to be high design standards and variety in size, layout and density. The statement established the need for segregation of development from through traffic, ample parking and garage facilities and the provision of adequate services. Distinctions were made between policies for inner area redevelopment and new outer development.

Physical design policies included: a high degree of conformity with many of the guidelines issued by the D.o.E. on space, lighting and insulation; specification of minimum garden sizes with exceptions for certain types of housing; provision of services, pedestrian movement, vehicle access and parking, together with children's play areas, to be approached with visual amenity and safety as guiding principles.

As far as visual design policies were concerned, the intention was to perpetuate the unique building character of Essex and re-establish local identity. New building was to have regard to the style, colour and texture of vernacular architecture and materials. The principle of spatial organisation for new buildings was to set them in a dominant landscape of a character which was indigenous to Essex or to have new built forms so organised as to enclose spaces of individual identity.

The Design Guide contained a section on case studies which included sketches, plans and models of layouts, elevations and photographs to help create an image of what it was hoped the new policies would achieve. The Report also contained detailed technical specifications to guide layout, design of buildings and landscaping.

Comment Many local authorities, such as Cheshire and Kent County Councils, followed Essex in producing guidelines as a means of preventing inappropriate development and to improve the quality of new developments. Not all reactions to design guides have been favourable and criticism includes the fear that patterns and styles of new development will simply repeat themselves throughout a county, resulting in the curtailing of architectural design, flair and creativity and an unwarranted extension of planning control over legitimate private sector development.

The Conservative Government (1979 onwards) has reservations about the 'reasonableness' of the planning systems imposing too many design constraints upon private developers engaged in new house building. In the D.o.E. Circular 22/80 the point is conceded that 'design guides may have a useful role to play provided they are used as guidance and not as detailed rules' and a clear warning is given to local authorities that they should not 'impose their tastes on developers' nor force them to 'adopt designs which are unpopular'.

References

Essex County Council (1973) *A Design Guide for Residential Areas*, County Council of Essex, Chelmsford

D.o.E. (1980) *Development Control — Policy and Practice*, Circular 22/80, HMSO, London

Owen, S. (1979) *Detailed Control and Guidance in Local Planning*, Gloucestershire Papers in Local Rural Planning, Issue no. 5, Department of Town and Country Planning, Gloucestershire Institute of Higher Education, Cheltenham

Tourism and Recreation Research Unit, University of Edinburgh Research Report No. 47 1981 The Economy of Rural Communities in the National Parks of England and Wales

Background The Report was commissioned in 1978, by the Countryside Commission, Department of Environment, English Tourist Board and Ministry of Agriculture, Fisheries and Food, with a remit to investigate the impact of National Park designation on resident communities and the contribution of these communities in helping to realise National Park objectives.

The research team was guided by an advisory group from sponsoring bodies and other pertinent agencies and organisations. The Report hoped to be of value to those involved in public policy-making and its implementation.

Findings The Report presented a wealth of information and detailed analysis which earlier reports had treated in outline only.

The Report concluded that it was possible to reconcile the traditional conflicts between conservation and development to the point where economic growth could be encouraged which would provide the basis for a healthy economy in National Parks without impairing the intrinsic characteristics of these designated areas.

There should be better guidance for those involved with National Parks by more co-ordination of the objectives of different government departments and through the establishment of inter-departmental committees, with the National Park Plan being accorded an appropriate status, and to which all public agencies operating in the Parks should conform.

The promotion of socio-economic welfare was recommended as a third statutory objective for National Parks.

There was a need to make assessments of landscape, economic and social opportunities, and the future use of the Parks for recreation and tourism as a basis for preparing more effective plans which would be accorded statutory status and include issues relating to socio-economic development. The Report also recommended

that a more effective machinery be established to ensure that plans were implemented.

Agriculture and forestry should be brought under limited planning control and financial aid to these industries should be governed by the objectives of particular National Parks in marked contrast to current practice.

There should be more positive attempts to promote appropriate additional economic activity through planning and the reorganisation and extension of financial assistance.

Comment Publication of the final Report was delayed for a considerable period by the Department of the Environment who were clearly unhappy about many of the recommendations because of the costs involved and by a Conservative administration (in office when the report was finally published) which found it difficult to accept the need for increased intervention.

The Report was widely supported by conservation groups and its detailed analysis provided added weight to the arguments advanced for a radical reappraisal of managing upland Britain in a number of major studies published in the early 1980s.

References

TRRU (1981) *The Economy of Rural Communities in the National Parks of England and Wales*, Tourism and Recreation Research Unit, Edinburgh

MacEwen, M. and Sinclair, G. (1983) *New Life for the Hills*, Council for National Parks, London

Berger, R. (1979) *The White Peak, a Study in Landscape Conservation*, Bartlett School of Architecture and Planning, London

Countryside Commission (1983) *What Future for the Uplands?*, Countryside Commission, Cheltenham

Council for National Parks 1983 New Life for the Hills

Background Following the intense debate of the Wildlife and Countryside Bill, the Council for National Parks determined to press for reform and reduce conflict between support for upland agriculture on the one hand and the growing public pressures to resist further landscape change in the uplands on the other. The basic concept was to seek ways of supporting the upland economy which could enhance rather than despoil and undermine landscape beauty and social fabric. Thus the Council commissioned a major research exercise to analyse and comment upon existing policies for upland areas and to make proposals for effective reform in government policies.

This report was seen as a direct sequel to the work of the Tourism and Recreation Research Unit at Edinburgh, and the book *National Parks: Conservation or Cosmetics?*

Findings The Report provided a background to the authors' concern about the uplands, central to which was the conflict between the operation of central government policies for agriculture and forestry and the need, as perceived by conservation and amenity groups, to give greater attention to conservation, amenity and recreation in the formulation of future agricultural and forestry policies for the uplands. It was also noted that successive governments had failed to take positive action on the recommendations made by the Countryside Review Committee on this issue.

The Report was concerned that changes and trends in land use and production were brought about or aggravated largely as a result of government agricultural policies. The Report therefore examined the impact of official policies on the physical, social and economic well-being of the uplands and concluded that UK and EEC policies had done little to provide a rational solution to the problems of farming in hill areas. They had in fact exacerbated social and economic problems in certain quarters and failed to create a situation in which new approaches to hill farming could be promoted without detriment to the economic interests of the farming community or the objectives of other interest groups in the countryside.

The Report identified the need for an alternative approach, involving the listing of objectives for a reformed set of policies for agriculture and forestry in the uplands. Strong emphasis would be placed on an integrated approach to reconcile good husbandry with conservation and the creation of stable conditions and new opportunities. The report considered a number of ideas which included reform of the Common Agricultural Policy to overcome the pressure on farmers to produce more and more and resource management incentives to strengthen the financial and non-financial incentives for conservation.

In looking at a number of options, such as leaving the system much as it was where strong vested interests prevail or the return to a free market system where all forms of incentive and aid to farmers would be withdrawn, the authors settled upon an integrated approach which would include reforms in headage payments, capital grant schemes, comprehensive and multi-purpose farm management plans, resource management incentives, comprehensive advisory services, together with some controls over agriculture and forestry. The authors saw the need to establish a trend towards rationality and consistency in respect of planning and aid for the uplands.

Comment The Report attempted to put forward reasonable and workable proposals — goals which are certainly achievable given sufficient political interest and landowner co-operation. Despite government interest in the reform of the Common Agricultural Policy, other issues clearly have higher priority and those with vested interests in maintaining the status quo remain an articulate, well-organised and powerful lobby group. An indication of wider government interest in the reform of policies in the uplands may come from any response made to the Countryside Commission's final statement on the Changing Uplands debate.

References

MacEwan, M. and Sinclair, G. (1983) *New Life for the Hills*, Council for National Parks, London

Sinclair, G. (1983) *Upland Landscapes Study*, Environment Information Services, London

TRRU (1981) *The Economy of Rural Communities in the National Parks of England and Wales*, Research Report no. 47, Tourism and Recreation Research Unit, Edinburgh

McEwen, A. and McEwen, M. (1982) *National Parks: Conservation or Cosmetics?*, George Allen and Unwin, London

POLICY INSTRUMENTS

Ministry of Housing and Local Government Circular 42/55 1955 Green Belts

Background Considerable concern had been expressed about uncontrolled urban sprawl in the inter-war period, a theme which continued to be debated in the post-war period. The ability to control development had been substantially increased by the development control powers introduced by the 1947 Town and Country Planning Act. This Green Belt circular was based on a Ministerial statement to the House of Commons in April 1955.

Findings The circular recognised three main reasons for establishing green belts: 'to check the further growth of built-up areas, to prevent neighbouring towns from merging into one another or to preserve the special character of a town'.

It argued the need for strict control on development in green belts: permission for development would be granted only in special circumstances. Overall, it was felt that there was a need to prevent further growth of towns and villages with a green belt.

Green belts were to be several miles wide to ensure a sizeable rural zone around built-up areas.

Comment Circular 42/55 has never been withdrawn and remains the cornerstone of government policy on green belts.

Since 1955 there has been considerable pressure for green belt land to be released for development and, despite attrition both at the edges and within green belts (statutory and non-statutory), they still remain as an important means for controlling outward urban growth.

Local planning control over green belts was transferred from county to district level in the cases of Greater London and the Metropolitan Counties as a direct result of Department of the Environment Circular 2/81, weakening strategic control of development in major urban areas.

The importance of recreation and amenity in green belts has never been emphasised in official ministry statements, despite their obvious potential for catering for many recreational and leisure pursuits of an urban-based population and despite the considerable amount of time and money that have been given over to promoting recreation and leisure in the urban fringe by both private and public bodies.

Although successive governments have remained committed to the concept of urban containment through green belt policies, there was some indication in the early 1980s of a weakening of Government resolve, perhaps as a result of pressure from the main housebuilding interests. In mid-1983 a new draft green belt circular was circulated for comment but was withdrawn in December, 1983, amidst a growing tide of protest and concern from within Parliament, local government, the Royal Town Planning Institute and many other pressure groups.

References
Ministry of Housing and Local Government (1955) *Green Belts*, Circular no. 42/55, HMSO, London
Munton, R. (1983) *London's Green Belt: Containment in Practice*, George Allen and Unwin, London
Thomas, D. (1970) *London's Green Belt*, Faber and Faber, London
Elson, M.J. (1979) *The Urban Fringe: Open Land Policies and Programmes in the Metropolitan Counties*, Countryside Commission Working Paper no. 14, Countryside Commission, Cheltenham

Town and Country Planning General Development Order 1977 (plus 1981 Amendment) Statutory Instrument No. 289 (plus No. 245)

Background Statutory Instruments such as the General Development Order are the means by which the Secretary of State for the Environment can make regulations under the Planning Act. Such regulations are laid before Parliament following the enactment of legislation and may be amended by the Secretary of State at any time — there does not have to be new legislation before any such amendment can take place.

Prior to the 1947 Town and Country Planning Act a number of Interim Development Orders were issued under the 1932 Town and Country Planning Act, but since the 1947 Act there have been a number of General Development Orders and Amendments.

The General Development Orders allow the Secretary of State to remove a significant number of small or trivial matters from the normal planning procedures by granting them automatic planning permission.

Findings At present, there are 24 Articles contained within the General Development Order covering a wide range of practical planning matters including interpretations of specific terms, issues pertaining to permitted development and restrictions upon permitted development (Article 4), development not in accordance with the Development Plan, procedures for consultation, application and notification, and appeals registers and certificates.

Under Schedule 1 of the General Development Order, there are listed 23 Classes of Permitted Development such as 'development within the curtilage of a dwelling house', 'agricultural buildings, works and uses', 'forestry buildings and works', 'development by statutory undertakers', and 'use as a caravan site'. Each of the classes contains a description of the development that is permissible and may include specific limitations — for example, the area of agricultural buildings shall not exceed 464 sq. metres (Class VI). In some cases additional conditions are included — for example, for many of the activities of statutory undertakers (Class XVIII) there is an obligation to remove all equipment and apparatus at the end of operations and restore land to its condition prior to development.

The Town and Country Planning General Development (Amendment) Order, 1981 (Statutory Instrument No. 245) introduced a limited number of changes to the 1977 General Development Order and of particular significance were amendments to certain class of 'permitted development'. There were certain relaxations in Class I 'Development within the curtilage of a dwelling house', Class III 'Changes of use' and Class VIII 'Development for industrial purposes'.

Comment Without the provisions of the General Development Orders considerable strain would have been placed upon planning machinery in the post-war period. Clearly recent changes in the General Development Order have further reduced some of the traditional work load on those involved with development control, particularly in respect of 'development within the curtilage of a dwelling use' and have given commercial and industrial operators more scope for change and expansion without requiring planning permission.

There are pressure groups, such as the Council for National Parks, which would undoubtedly prefer to see Class VI 'Agricultural, buildings, works and uses' removed from the General Development Order to give planning authorities greater control over development in sensitive rural areas. It remains true that many people involved directly in the planning process are concerned that recent amendments to the General Development Order might herald a further relaxation of statutory control over development.

References
HM Government (1977) *The Town and Country Plan-*

ning General Order, Statutory Instrument no. 289, HMSO, London
HM Government (1981) *The Town and Country Planning General Development (Amendment) Order*, Statutory Instrument no. 245, HMSO, London
Ratcliffe, J. (1981) *An Introduction to Town and Country Planning*, Hutchinson, London

Town and Country Planning General Development Order 1977
Article 4, Statutory Instrument No. 289

Background Under the General Development Order, there are a number of classes of development which do not require planning permission and are termed 'permitted development'. If the Secretary of State for the Environment, or a local planning authority in conjunction with the Secretary of State, feel that for special reasons deemed permission for development under the General Development Order should be withdrawn for a particular category or a chosen area, this can be done by issuing an Article 4 Direction.

Findings Directions made under Article 4 of the General Development Order can be made by either the Secretary of State or the local planning authority, and in most circumstances a Direction made by the local planning authority will require the approval of the Secretary of State for the Environment. This he may do with or without modification.

Article 4 lays down procedures for the notification of owners and occupiers of every part of the land affected by any Direction made under this Article. This can be done individually or, where the planning authority deem it to be more appropriate, by publishing a notice in the local press and the London Gazette. The Direction takes effect when notification has taken place.

Any Direction made under Article 4 may be withdrawn at a later stage and in most cases approval must be sought by the local planning authority from the Secretary of State and notice must again be given to all owners and occupiers in the land affected.

There are circumstances under which the Direction shall have no effect, namely in respect of development in the case of emergency or specified operations carried out by statutory undertakers.

Comment The issuing of Article 4 Directions is accepted practice in conservation areas and Areas of Outstanding Natural Beauty. In his review of the development control system, Dobry felt that there was more scope for the use of Article 4 Directions to give local authorities the flexibility to use this form of control in response to particular local needs.

There are important cases where local planning authorities have failed to persuade the appropriate minister of the need to make a Direction under Article 4 — witness the attempts of Exmoor National Park to have the fencing of parts of Exmoor brought under planning control.

Although Article 4 Directions are a valuable planning tool and have been used to good effect in the past, in the light of relaxations in the control of development by the Conservative Government since 1979, it is unlikely that there will be any significant increase in approvals by the Secretary of State.

References

HM Government (1977) 'Article 4, Directions Restricting Development', part of HM Government, *The Town and Country Planning General Development Order 1977*, Statutory Instrument no. 289, HMSO, London

Ratcliffe, J. (1981) *An Introduction to Town and Country Planning*, Hutchinson, London

Blacksell, M. and Gilg, A. (1981) *The Countryside: Planning and Change*, George Allen and Unwin, London

Department of the Environment Circular 22/80
1980
Development Control — Policy and Practice

Background This circular was issued in response to a growing tide of Conservative Party and Government feeling that planning was working against the interests of economic initiatives, development and recovery. There was concern that many planning policies were overly restrictive, the system inflexible and procedures too slow and often cumbersome.

Findings There were two main aims of the circular: to secure a general speeding up of the planning system and to ensure development is only restricted when this serves clear planning purpose (and when all economic effects have been taken into account).

A variety of suggestions were made in respect of speed and efficiency, such as the use of delegated powers, shorter committee cycles, efficient arrangements for all necessary consultations and the prompt notification of decisions taken. The implication of lack of promptness, relevance and efficiency were spelt out in terms of destroying confidence in investment for new development vital to economic recovery.

The circular identified a number of issues which have caused controversy and delay, such as alternative uses for historic buildings and issues relating to aesthetic control. Planning authorities should be more flexible in dealing with change of use for historic buildings and to consider an economic future for them. Planning authorities should recognise that aesthetics are an extremely subjective matter and should not seek to impose their own standards unnecessarily upon developers. The need for stricter control in sensitive areas such as National Parks was acknowledged by the view that control over the external appearance of buildings should only be exercised where there were indisputable reasons for doing so.

The circular attempted to allay any fears about a lessening of safeguards in sensitive areas such as National Parks and green belt areas and noted that no more than an essential minimum of agricultural land would be taken for development. Where possible, poorer land should be used in preference to higher grades.

Of the annexes attached to the circular, the one entitled 'Planning Permission for Private Sector House Building' was of relevance to countryside planning, particularly the paragraphs dealing with 'constraints on development', 'supply of land', 'extension of urban development into the countryside', and 'development in villages'. The circular accepted the need for planning authorities to identify a five-year supply of land for housing. If this was not available, there should be a presumption in favour of granting permission for housing except where there were acceptable reasons for not doing so, such as the presence of other overriding policies (National Park, green belt, Area of Outstanding Natural Beauty, quality of agricultural land). Before outward expansion of towns was permitted, the circular stated that unused land within towns should be fully utilised and that if there were no alternatives, then ribbon development should be avoided as should land covered by other national policies. It was accepted that some villages had reached the full extent of natural growth, but that in others there was still some capacity.

Comment The circular has generated much concern in planning circles that hard-won principles will be thrown over in favour of pragmatic responses to development and that, in the longer term, planning control will be undermined and its contribution to society as a whole weakened.

Although there appear to be a number of safeguards to the rural environment contained within this circular, many groups would argue that development control powers in the countryside should be strengthened and extended to encompass agricultural and forestry activities.

References

Department of the Environment (1980) *Development Control — Policy and Practice*, Circular no. 22/80, HMSO, London

Herington, J. (1982) 'Circular 22/80 — the demise of Settlement Planning?', *Area*, vol. 14, pp. 157-66

Notes on Contributors

John Blunden is Reader in Geography at the Open University. A graduate in social studies from the University of Exeter, his doctoral thesis investigated spatial and temporal variations in the impact of agricultural support policies on farm enterprises. After working as a BBC producer, he returned to academic life through a fellowship at the University of Sussex. Since then his research interests in resource management have been reflected in a wide range of books and papers.

Henry Buller is currently a researcher at the Department of Town Planning, Oxford Polytechnic. Prior to this he worked at King's College in the University of London on local amenity politics which was the subject of his doctoral thesis. He is presently investigating the conflicts between motorised sports in the countryside and conservation.

Louise Catchpole is a lecturer in the Law Department of the University of Reading. After studying in London and at the University of Oxford for her first and post-graduate degrees in Law she began her teaching career at Nottingham University. Although she has an interest in family law and the law of evidence, she has maintained a particular concern for planning law.

Nigel Curry is Senior Lecturer in Countryside Planning at Gloucestershire College of Arts and Technology. He holds degrees in economics and in agricultural economics and completed his PhD on recreation economics in the Land Economy Department at the University of Cambridge. He has published several articles on economic issues relating to the countryside.

Philip Lowe has degrees in natural science, science policy and history. He is Lecturer in Countryside Planning at University College in the University of London and has written extensively in the fields of countryside planning, rural sociology, environmental politics and the history of ecology.

Alan Rogers is Lecturer in Countryside Planning at Wye College in the University of London. His main area of research concerns rural housing, which was also the subject of his doctoral thesis. He is particularly involved with the voluntary sector in rural community development and is presently Chairman of the Standing Conference of Rural Community Councils.

Tim Shaw read Geography at Edinburgh University. He has held appointments as a lecturer in geography at Ahmadu Bello University, Nigeria and in the Department of Town and Country Planning, Liverpool Polytechnic. He is now Lecturer in Countryside Planning at the University of Newcastle upon Tyne where he has research interests in aspects of natural resource exploitation and environmental impact assessment.

[library stamp, illegible]